Credos and Curios

Books by James Thurber
available in Harper paperback editions

Alarms and Diversions
Fables for Our Times
Lanterns and Lances
My Life and Hard Times
The Thurber Carnival
Is Sex Necessary? *(with E. B. White)*

Credos and Curios

James Thurber

HARPER COLOPHON BOOKS
Harper & Row, Publishers
New York, Cambridge, Philadelphia, San Francisco
London, Mexico City, São Paulo, Sydney

"Carpe Noctem, If You Can" appeared originally in the *Atlantic Monthly;* "Return of the Native" and "Look Out for the Thing" in *The Bermudian;* "Afternoon of a Playwright" in *Esquire;* "The Other Room," "The Future, If Any, of Comedy" and "The Danger in the House" in *Harper's Magazine;* "The Real Man, Nugent" in the *New York Times;* "The Incomparable Mr. Benchley" in the *New York Times Book Review;* "The Notebooks of James Thurber," "Menaces in May," "Six for the Road" and "The Manic in the Moon" in *The New Yorker;* "Brother Endicott" in *Playboy;* "Scott in Thorns" in *The Reporter;* "E.B.W." in the *Saturday Review;* "The Man Who Was Comedy" in *Theatre Arts;* "The Lady from the Land" ("Cocktail Party Line") in *Town and Country.*

"My Friend McNulty" was included in *The World of John McNulty* by John McNulty, published by Doubleday; "Mary Petty and Her Drawings" in *This Petty Pace* by Mary Petty, published by Knopf; and "Foreword to the Fifth New Yorker Album" in *The Fifth New Yorker Album,* published by Harper.

A hardcover edition of this book was published by Harper & Row, Publishers, Inc.

CREDOS AND CURIOS. Copyright © 1928, 1938, 1940, 1945, 1948, 1949, 1951, 1957, 1961, 1962 by Helen Thurber. Copyright 1949 by James Thurber. Copyright 1932 by Harper & Row, Publishers. All rights reserved. Printed in the United States of America. No part of this book may be used or reproduced in any manner whatsoever without written permission except in the case of brief quotations embodied in critical articles and reviews. For information address Harper & Row, Publishers, Inc., 10 East 53rd Street, New York, N.Y. 10022. Published simultaneously in Canada by Fitzhenry & Whiteside Limited, Toronto.

First HARPER COLOPHON edition published 1983.

Library of Congress Cataloging in Publication Data

Thurber, James, 1894-1961.
    Credos and curios.

    (Harper colophon books ; CN/1018)
    I. Title.
PS3539.H94C7 1983   818'.5209   82-48236
ISBN 0-06-091018-6 (pbk.)

83 84 85 86 10 9 8 7 6 5 4 3 2 1

They shall have stars at elbow and foot; . . .
And death shall have no dominion.

And death shall have no dominion. . . .

DYLAN THOMAS

Contents

~~~~~~~~~~

Foreword

ᎧᎧᎧᎧᎧᎧᎧᎧᎧᎧᎧ

Among the scattered notes that I found after my husband's death were a few sheets of yellow paper, covered
with his familiar and almost illegible scrawl and listing
future pieces and projects. (He was always less interested
in what he had done than in what he planned to do.) On
one sheet, alone and looking very lonely, were the words
"Credos and Curios." Another contained the contents page
of what was to be his next book. With these two sheets as
my guide, I have put together, as far as I was able, this
collection.

I say "as far as I was able" because some of the pieces on
the list were never finished, and some, alas, existed only in
my husband's mind and memory. I shall always be sorry
that he never got around to writing "An Evening with
Hemingway," "Shake Hands with Sinclair Lewis," and
"Cocktails with Thomas Wolfe" (a memorable night that
ended at eight in the morning). I was lucky enough, if that
is the right word, and I don't think it is, to be present on
all three occasions, and the story of what went on deserved
to be recorded.

I am even sorrier that the glorious tale of Miss Naddy's Dancing Academy of Columbus, Ohio, was never put on paper. This was a favorite Thurber recitation, told with nostalgic relish, and I will never forget the picture of that dancing class, over a bowling alley very much on the wrong side of the tracks, and so delightfully different from the prim, white-gloved school where I learned to one-step. At Miss Naddy's (forgive me if I misspell her name—I have only heard it spoken), most of the male students smoked cigars and packed guns, but their teacher was pretty tough herself, and never daunted. "All right, now we'll try another moonlight waltz," she would yell, after three previous attempts by candlelight had failed, ending in what could hardly be called waltzing, "and this time I want you guys to stay out from behind them palms!"

Except for these pieces, I have kept closely to my husband's contents page for his book, and have given it his own stray and solitary title. He may never have meant it for a book at all, but it seems curiously to fit this varied collection of pieces. Quite a few of them express in some way his credos—his beliefs and feelings about humor and comedy, for example. Others, such as the Prefaces and short profiles of people he knew and admired, could be called Curios since they fit into no particular pattern. My husband had for a long time wanted to bring these small tributes together in one volume, so here they are. Some of the facts in them may seem a little out of date, but his admiration for the people had no limitations in time.

Dates have been added wherever they seemed significant. This was especially important in the case of "Menaces in May," definitely a period piece, with more than a touch of juvenilia, but interesting because it was the first Thurber story in *The New Yorker* to depart from the "little funny casual" he was writing in those early days. That makes it a kind of landmark, and to many people at the time it showed the promise later to be developed in such stories as "One Is a Wanderer" and "The Evening's at Seven." I've always been happy that James Thurber was a writer of humor— God knows we need them, as he often pointed out—but I am even happier that he was more than that.

To those who may feel that a few of the recent pieces, written during the last year of my husband's life, reveal some bitterness and disillusion with the world, I can only say that in this period his own favorite book was that realistic message of hope, *The Last Flower*, and that it was not too long before his death that he wrote the lines: "Let us not look back in anger, nor forward in fear, but around in awareness." He showed all three at times—anger certainly, fear perhaps—but he always put awareness above the others. That, I think, is the real key to James Thurber as a person and as a writer.

HELEN THURBER

July 17, 1962

1

The Notebooks of James Thurber

ccccccccccccccccccccccccccccccccccccccccc

I explained many years ago why my letters will probably
never be collected and published under the title "I Saw It
Coming," or under any other title. Since you have no doubt
forgotten what I had to say, I will sketch it in for you
briefly. I came back from Europe in 1938 to discover that
my friends had not saved my letters—or "preserved the
correspondence," to use the formal phrase. Oh, they had
preserved it in a manner of speaking, but they "couldn't
put their hands on it at the moment." That is, they didn't
have the vaguest idea where it was. I knew where it was
then, and I know where it is now. Letters have a way of
ending up in attics and warehouses, along with polychrome
bookends, masquerade costumes, copies of the *American
Mercury* for 1930, and Aunt Martha's water colors of Blois
and Chenonceaux. If my friends ever set out to locate my
letters, they will come upon old college yearbooks, dance
programs, snapshot albums, and the works of John Fox,
Jr., and probably lose interest in the original object of their
search.

Now, the seventy-one letters written from abroad in 1937-38 were intended as a section of the collected correspondence to be called *Part III: The European Phase,* and their unavailability is regarded by my publishers as a "major deterrent." As for *Part I: The Youthful Years* and *Part II: Sturm und Drang (1915-1935),* God only knows what has become of the letters written during those so important formative periods. There remain the letters written since 1938, and while they are "as available as hell," to quote one of my attorneys, their publication would not constitute "an act of wisdom," to quote him further. These letters repose in the files of producers, publishers, editors, and agents, and their monotony is another major deterrent, since they all begin with "As God is my judge" or "I would rather die than" and trail off into vague hints or open threats of legal action. After reading my carbons of this correspondence, my publishers wrote me as follows: "I am afraid that we are all of one mind here in feeling that what had every sign of a swell performance has now turned into a rather dark picture. Mr. Steckley, of our legal department, is especially distressed, but he is perhaps a bit intemperate in estimating that defamation suits in the amount of $3,000,000 would result from the publication of *Part IV: The Challenging Years.* We hope you may have a jolly fairy tale up your sleeve—something about giants and little princesses."

The middle-aged, or, as he prefers to be called, mature, writer who realizes that his *Collected Letters* (2 vols., $10) are never going to be brought out sooner or later hits on the idea of gathering together his notes—memoranda, plot outlines, descriptions of characters, and fragments of philosophy—and seeing if he can't do something with them. He is now treading on ground hallowed by the

Thurber and his Circle.

important notebooks of the great masters, from da Vinci to Henry James, but if his invention is running low and his taxes are high, he will go brashly ahead with his ill-advised project. This instantly marks him as a minor author. The notebooks of a major author are always brought out after his death, by a literary executor. If you are a major author, the literary executor will hang around your house, known as "the estate," for at least a year, mousing through voluminous papers, collating and annotating, drinking your Scotch with your widow, and sometimes, in the end, marrying your daughter.

There is also the disturbing chance that your executor, while mousing around in your literary remains, may stumble on the Figure in the Carpet, or what he conceives to be the Figure in the Carpet. That is, he may adduce from the notebooks dubious internal evidence supporting the theory that you were homosexual, impotent, or secretly in love with your radio agent's wife. It will be up to your daughter, then, to marry your executor and shut him up, but, if she is a Vassar graduate, she may collaborate with him on a sequel to the notebooks—*The Real John Marcher,* an honest, courageous, and best-selling examination, on behalf of the enrichment of American letters— that will strip you of every last posthumous pride and privacy. If you are a major author, and all this has frightened you, I suggest that you remove from your notebooks everything that might be regarded as evidence of "the scar"; that is, the early trauma, illness, maladjustment, or inadequacy that led you to become a writer in the first place. Or it might be simpler just to send your daughter to Cornell.

The minor author, known in New York merely as "a writer" and in Hollywood as "a word man," comes to his typewriter with few, if any, notes to guide him. He may jot down a phrase or two on the back of an envelope in a taxi or on a bus, but such notes are usually thrown away as soon as a piece is finished. Even if they were preserved, an accumulation of them over a period of years would scarcely occupy one afternoon of a serious literary executor, who would classify them as "unr.," which means "unrewarding" and suitable only as mementos for hotel maids, assistant gardeners, and third cousins.

If only to justify the title of this essay, I began to poke around one day to see what I could find in the way of memoranda and memorabilia of my own. What I came up with presents a very dark picture indeed, complete with at least seven major deterrents: persistent illegibility, paucity of material, triviality of content, ambiguity of meaning, facetious approach, preponderance of juvenilia, and exasperating abbreviation. There is actually only one notebook, and since it is the solidest, or at any rate the heaviest, item in the collection, we should perhaps glance at it first. It is a notebook I kept, or was supposed to keep, in Professor Weiss's psychology class at Ohio State University in 1913. The first few pages are given over to a description of the medulla oblongata, a listing of the primary colors, the score of the Western Reserve–Ohio State football game that season, and the words "Noozum, Noozum, Noozum." (I figured out this last entry after some thought. There was a young woman in the class named Newsome, whom Dr. Weiss always called Noozum.) The rest of the pages contain a caricature of Professor Weiss; one hundred and thirteen swastikas; the word "Noozum" in block letters; the notation "No William James in library"; an address, 1374 Summit Street; a memo: "drill cap, white gloves, gym suit. See G. Packer.

Get locker"; a scrawl that seems to read "Orgol lab nor fot Thurs"; and a number of horrible two-line jokes, which I later contributed to the *Sundial,* the university monthly magazine. Two of these will more than suffice:

(1) HE: The news from Washington is bad.
      SHE: I thought he died *long* ago.

(2) ADMIRAL WATCHING ENEMY SINK: Who fired that shot?
      MATE: The ship's cook, sir. He got the range and stove in her side.

No literary executor is going to get his hands on *that* notebook.

I am sorry to say that this rather vacant item is the most orderly exhibit in the pitiful clump of notes I have been able to discover. Most of my other material is written in pencil on sheets of yellow copy paper that have been folded over twice, a practice common with newspaper reporters but highly irritating to literary executors. Let us take the notes in order.

The first sheet, then, bears the following, in pencil, near the top of the upper left quarter: "Digital. b. donna. stramoneum (Jimson weed). Horn quicksilver. Germander. Aloes. Aloes yourself." The flippancy of the final phrase, "Aloes yourself," suggests that the piece to which this note obviously has reference was not written in a serious mood. Either that or the author's mood changed between the time he made the note and the time he actually wrote the piece.

We come now to the longest of the notes, and the only one with a sense of affirmation. There are twenty-five sheets here, one of them stained with cider, perhaps, and all of them folded only once. The pages are not dated; nothing ever is. The chirography has a curious smudged or

sat-on appearance; there are only twenty words to a page, and again the author's mood and intent seem ambiguous. The manuscript that grew out of this plot summary was blown out to sea from a Hamilton-bound ferryboat just off Watford Bridge, Bermuda, on April 8, 1947. There was, of course, no carbon copy. Certain editorial symbols have been employed for purposes of clarification, and where words were not clear, they have, quite simply, been guessed at. Question marks have been parenthesized after such words. Perhaps the reader will wish to hazard interpretations of his own. That is his privilege. The notes, in full, follow:

7

"Middle-aged novelist has been unable to think of anything to write about for eleven years. Name Julian Gordon. Julian picks up copy Harpers Bazzaar (sic) at Tass (?) agency, reads swell short story signed Candace Poe. It turns out to be work of Mr. Gordon's wife, who's been secretly knitting little plots. He can't stand having his wife writing without help from him. Julian sarcastically says no female writes without using 'it was as if' all the time. Real rift begins when he finds her hangout over garage and reads sheet in ivory-colored typewriter. Tells her at dinner she can't use sentence 'The wind ran scampering up the street like a laughing boy.' You've got to use either 'ran' or 'scampered.' Rift widens. Cath. says she is going to re-name their country place Greensleeves because look nice on station wagon door. He says by God over his dead body. 15 collar 33 or 34 sleeve B. Brothers blue button-down. Sox 11½. (Note: This appears to be a personal memo, without reference to the plot outline.) Julian, who is still on Ch. 6 of novel begun 1936, discovers Cath. has sold several pieces to mags. in one month, and is in correspondence with Cerf, Finkelhoff (?), and Warner Bros. Julian Gordon announces he intends to buy Smith & Wesson .38 police special on ground that everybody under 21 is out to get him. Sees wife thinks he is going crazy, and decides play part of maniac to hilt. Says sees large silver fish float through bedroom. Says hears horns of elfland f.b. Says Louise Glaum (?) keeps phoning. Cath. buys vicious fawn-colored boxer as protection against J. Wonderful scene in garage studio while cleaning gun and she typing and boxer growling. She certain he intends shoot her 'accidentally.' Cath. suddenly cries, 'Get him, Greensleeves!' She has called boxer Greensleeves, and now sets him on Gordon Julian (sic). Nuts to Gordon nuts to Cath. nuts to you nuts to me." That is all there is to the only really interesting item in the Thurber collection.

There are a few more odds and ends, or, to be exact, odds and beginnings, but we need scrutinize only three. The first goes, "The beaver is a working fool, who went to manual-training school." I have never been able to fit this in anywhere. The second says, "Guinea pigs fight when empty milk bottles are clicked together." They do, too. The third reads, "The American Woman. $1,300 emerald cigarette lighter." Since the word "woman" is capitalized, this obviously does not refer to any particular woman to whom I intended to give a thirteen-hundred-dollar emerald cigarette lighter. Furthermore, I haven't got that kind of money. There was probably an idea for a story in this note when I set it down, but I don't see it now. If you do, you can have it—the idea, I mean. The note itself has been destroyed, along with everything else, except the plot outline of *Greensleeves*. I should take a swing at that story again, now that the fawn-colored boxer is all the rage.

2

Menaces in May

ᏯᏯᏯᏯᏯᏯᏯᏯᏯᏯᏯᏯᏯᏯᏯᏯᏯᏯᏯᏯ

The lights of the Hotel Belgium's lank electric sign in West Forty-seventh Street go out at one o'clock. The side of the Palace Theatre across the street looms up then like a dark hill. Two doors away glow the lights of the Somerset delicatessen, open all night. Farther toward Sixth Avenue a little green door swings open and shut incessantly and men bustle in and other men stumble out. Across Sixth Avenue Brentano's and its neighbors are chastely asleep and the street is as tranquil as a road in a suburb.

To the man standing at a window on the fifth floor of the Belgium, the prospect is new and interesting. He watches the vaudeville people coming out of the Somerset, their sharp pantomime blurred by a steady rain. The chap in the very gray suit is obviously mimicking Ted Lewis. A girl takes his gesticulating arm and laughs. Four men stand in a group by the curb, talking loudly, waving their hands: probably dismissing someone as lousy—a noted performer perhaps, or all stage managers.

The sound of a quartet singing on a phonograph record, "Dear, on a Night Like This," comes from the room the man is in, and he turns away from the window. Joe is muffling the Victrola by stuffing a towel into it, because it is so late. Julia is sitting on the edge of the bed. She doesn't say anything when Joe asks her where the devil the fibre needles are. Joe, the man notices, has become a little fat and his hair is thinning. Julia is exactly the same as eighteen years ago. The man ponders the little miracle of their meeting tonight. He had turned an unfamiliar corner and there they were. Julia, as lovely as ever, laughing in the rain. Once they had all been in an Ohio grammar school together. Now they had met on a silly corner in New York, in the rain, at midnight. Perfectly swell the way things happen. Probably everything in life is arranged that way: precise, ineluctable, like a Jed Harris play. "What a day was yes-ter-day for yes-ter-day gave me you-u-u." Joe admires the way Gene Austin sings. He's marvellous, isn't he? What? Oh, yes, wonderful. Isn't he now? Marvellous. Joe is hunting for something again. Where the devil is "Mary Ann"—you got to hear the saxophone in that. The man remembers that Joe had always been importunate, restless like this. The man had been shy, "smart at his lessons." One doesn't win Julias that way. Is one sorry about that? The man looks down into the street again. Funny, now he is writing plays and Joe and Julia are dancing together. Vaudeville. What would that be like? A blonde lady comes out of the Somerset finishing a sandwich. Swiss cheese with lotsa mustard probably. How the devil could Julia be so untouched by all that sort of thing? Was she? Well, what if she wasn't? "And then—my heart —stood—still . . ."

His heart too stands still. Does something, anyway. When she puts her hand to her hair like that. The first gesture he had ever been stricken forlorn by. His mother used to laugh about it. Puppy love. How he had hated that! "Deep as first love and wild with all regret." . . . What? Oh, yes, swell saxophone. That's Red Nichols—great, isn't he? Great. How the mechanics of music affect Joe! He doesn't seem to hear the words. "We'll always be-e-e to-geth-er . . ." Julia rises and lifts the needle. What's the matter with that? Oh, play something lively, Joe. *That's* lively! Wonder what Julia's life with him is like. Wonder what his own life with Julia would have been. Hers with him. "Every daisy—in the dell—seems to know—but they won't tell—Mary Ann . . ." Joe sings with the record. He can sing. "I'll be yours—say you'll be mine—Mary Ann." Joe goes over and kisses her. The man stirs quickly. Joe keeps his arm around her. The man moves about. It's terribly late. He must go. It's three o'clock. One more drink. Well, all right. Here's Happiness. . . .

The man leaves, goes down in the elevator, out into the street. Happiness . . . What a nice thing life is. He sees his image in the elevator mirrors grinning at him. Good Lord, he's acting like a youngster in love. Well, what of it? It's wonderful. He starts to hum. ". . . for yes-ter-day gave me you-u-u." On the way out of the hotel he notices the sign he had laughed about when they came in: Permanent—Transient. One word. Lot in that. Or is there? Permanent. Odd, the word seems strange and meaningless when you study it. He thinks abruptly of Lydia. Lydia is away . . . Lydia has been away a long time . . . Lydia. . . . Funny, that name sounds unfamiliar too when you keep saying it. He remembers how he used to do that when he was a boy, keep saying words till they sounded crazy. Wife. Wife. *That* sounds crazy. Husband. Meals. All that sounds crazy. . . . "What a day was yes-ter-day . . ."

More lights go out in the street. Stragglers march by like

12

worn soldiers bringing up the frayed and awful edge of battle. Someone shouts a tremendous curse that rolls down the street like an iron wheel. Someone else falls sprawling, his overcoat flapping out on both sides. It is dark and a little cold and the rain is relentless. There is the dull morose thunder of ashcans being shoved and rolled and dropped, the ponderous noises of after three o'clock. They are pulling the stupid sleepy city onto its feet for another day. A taxi rides up with its melancholy clacking rhythms, shrieks as it slows down, groans, and rides on.

A sharp sense of menace strikes the man as he turns into Times Square. Men walk with a creeping tread at three o'clock on a wet morning along Broadway. They lurch toward you with sinister suddenness and no word. The sound of a scuffle comes out of a doorway and a choking curse: two cops appear dragging a young fellow between them. His hat is smashed on his head, his face leers up all covered with blood. The cops are breathing hard and grinning grimly. The young fellow gasps short horrible words. They hit him and go on around a corner, dragging him. In their wake a cluster of men pronounce judgment in wisecracks. One of them wears a strangely prim pair of nose glasses.

Times Square is a deserted circus ground. The splendor of lights and the fifty thousand people have passed in a few ticks of the clock. A dozen wanderers move about like sick clowns left behind. Two men, dressed too neatly in clothes that are too tight, walk past close to the man. One talks without moving his lips. "By god I bin gettin' something on this bird for two years and now by god I'm goin' t' get him." "Pipe down fa cry sake, ya wanta tell the world about it?" They glance at the man. Thank God he didn't overhear them name anyone. Mike Zerrelli—it would have been some meaningless name like that. He shudders and passes along quickly.

Stalking figures clack out a death watch waiting for the express at Times Square. Someone plays the chocolate and Spearmint machines with all the pennies he has. A girl laughs loudly under a sailor's jaw. In New York you never see sailors where sailors belong. Sailors are always in the subway. She stares incessantly at the sailor's eyes, fingering his blouse. He doesn't look at her and his small grin is fixed. He'll probably slip out at Seventy-second Street just as the door starts to close and she'll ride on a dozen stops farther, bitterly silent, chewing gum.

The downtown local gets to Times Square first. The local is asprawl with sleeping men. Incongruously upright men are fascinated by the decay of sleep. Mouths drop agape, a hat rolls dustily onto the floor, a man's jaw hits his knee and he sits up with an impossibly quick regaining

14

of his senses. In an impossibly brief while he sags again. A lean man, very drunk, gets on at the Pennsylvania Station. He is as menacing as a flung knife. He kicks the hat that lies on the floor, sits down too quickly beside a drowsing workman, cuffs off the workman's hat. "Whatta hell's matta you?" the insulted one mumbles. "Yeah, whatta hell's matta *you*?" says the drunken one. "Ya ever bin in love ya ever bin in love the hell ya ever bin in love the hell ya have. . . ."

The man gets off at Fourteenth, goes out the Thirteenth Street exit. He steps around a puddle of dark water and shivers. He remembers that a month ago a Cuban robbed a poolroom nearby, fled with eight dollars, shot a man through the heart, killed him, ran madly down into the subway, into the exit, beat against the spiked iron gate. "Hey! You can't get through that way, mister!" a youngster cried. A cop loomed at the top stair. The Cuban shot himself through the head. He had killed a man. The morning papers told how the man he had killed wasn't killed at all because he carried a Columbian half dollar for luck in his vest pocket and that saved him. Someone is whistling at the top of the steps tonight. "Spare a guy a dime, brother?" The man gives him a handful of coins and hurries on. His heart is beating fast. "I'm a damn coward." He remembers Lord Jim and how bravely he died. Well, Lord Jim had a reason to die. People cried about Lord Jim, he supposed. What the devil, it was a perfect death, his own inevitable end. Nothing hard about that. It's the dread of your life being ended for no reason—for no reason "On a Night Like This." That was it. Take Cyrano. Someone hit Cyrano on the head with a chimney brick or something. "I have missed everything, even my own death," Cyrano said. That's the menace, missing your own end—your own third act. "I'm

15

not a coward." The man goes on whistling.

He clicks the door of his room behind him and leans heavily against the door. What the devil has been the matter with him? It was because of meeting Julia. That was it. Chaos had threatened a perfectly directed evening. Maybe his life even. . . . He finds himself abruptly standing in front of one of the old bronze candelabra Lydia brought home from France. A breeze from an open window stirs in the room. He can see Lydia's fingers moving in and out of the tinkling crystal pendants, arranging the slim pink candles. What was that poem of Lizette Reese's? "Lydia's been gone this many a year, but the house is full of her." Something like that. The house is full of her. It always is. Even this long while she's been gone. She'll be back in a week now. . . .

Suddenly he is getting out some pictures. Here is Lydia in April sunlight, when she was eighteen. Lydia in college, Lydia feeding the silly gulls at Nice, Lydia in a snow of lavender crocuses at Saint Martin Vesubie—that had been in May—two, Lord, three years ago. Lydia on a hillside across from Saint Paul du Var that Sunday when they listened to the ancient bells of the town over the valley. What a finely wrought thing they had made of life. Lovely as a design in crystal, but strong as life. How strong was that? Supposing that sailor in the subway had started to choke the girl. You'd be a coward if you didn't do something, wouldn't you? It's heroic to try to save a life; any life, a sordid, senseless, alien life. A man doesn't run. No, he would have had to stick it out and be stabbed by a lecherous sailor. The papers would have run his picture and said what he did was fine. Fine! Lydia would have come home to *that*. But what a swell thing it was after all to walk on the high thin edge of irony and snap your

16

fingers at an alien and nameless terror. Snap your fingers. He hadn't snapped his fingers. He had been scared to death. Because of Lydia. He smiles, not knowing just why.

He gets undressed and goes to bed. The thunder of cans being dropped and the flash of bitter phrases ring through his mind. He tries to keep his mind fixed on the dark sheen of a whirling Victrola record. "What a day was yes-ter-day for yes-ter-day gave me you-u-u . . . the hell ya ever bin in love the hell ya bin in love the hell ya have . . ."

May, 1928

3

Six for the Road

ᴠᴠᴠᴠᴠᴠᴠᴠᴠᴠᴠᴠᴠᴠᴠᴠᴠᴠᴠᴠᴠ

Providence, no less, guided me to a question-and-answer department in a Sunday newspaper some time ago. I say Providence because the problem posed by a worried hostess that day should have been presented to me in the first place, and not to the etiquette editor, whoever she is. She may know more than I will ever know about silverware and napery, what flowers to put in a finger bowl, and how to write a letter of condolence to an estranged niece-in-law, but when it comes to the etiquette of the stirrup cup, or nightcap, she is palpably beyond her depth.

Before I proceed further, it might be well to quote the question and answer that Providence brought to my attention, so you will know what I am talking about. Here, then, they are, in full:

LATE STAYERS

QUESTION: "We have some very good friends whom we like to see, but they always stay too late in the evening. Is there any way we can avoid this without being rude?"

ANSWER: "The husband who has to get up early can excuse himself and go to bed, or his wife might say, 'John dear, you go to bed—you have to be up early tomorrow morning.' The

18

guests will then probably leave. If they do not, the wife will have to sit up with them."

Now, I have no doubt that these helpful hints will work splendidly in the case of the sherry set, or with the people on the genteel, or Malaga, fringe of our society. They could also be successfully applied to those ladies and gentlemen who take one brandy after dinner and then settle for a single highball in order to have something to hold, rather than to drink, but bringing these rules to bear, say, on the Harry Spencers and *their* circle would be like trying to make quicksilver stick to a window pane.

Let us try the formula on Harry and Joan Spencer at an evening party and see what happens or, to be precise, what doesn't happen. (By evening party, I mean, of course, one that begins in the afternoon and ends in the morning.) On this occasion, the Spencers' victims—or host and hostess, if you insist on being archaic—are Jim and Laura Bloodgood. The Bloodgoods had met the Spencers at a party in Rye two weeks before, and had asked them, along with some of their other friends, to cocktails and a buffet supper. Jim and Laura had been fascinated by Harry's stories and Joan's fresh charm. Jim had been particularly delighted by Harry's Sam Langford anecdotes and by his famous account of his experiences in a camouflage unit during the war.

The night of the Bloodgoods' party is not one of Jim's best nights, as luck would have it. Laura has even tried to get him to call it off, but he won't listen. He insists that Harry Spencer will be good for him, will cheer him up, and he can stand a lot of cheering up. Jim is a publisher, and things have not been going too well. In September, he developed an irritating stomach rash that his young doctor, hivey from an allergy of his own, diagnosed as psychosomatic. The doctor said he didn't think Bloodgood's rash would disappear until production costs eased off a bit.

Early in the evening, when Jim is discussing his ailment, Harry Spencer wows everybody, except his host, with the remark "The seventy-year itch, eh, Bloodgood?" It is at this point that the high tide of Jim's interest in the Spencers (Joan had led the laughter) begins to ebb. It is to ebb further a moment later, when Harry begins to harp amiably on Jim Bloodgood's sorest point, the failure of a book he had published entitled *They Ain't Nobody Here but Us Chickens,* merrily written by a young woman during six months on a poultry farm with her city-bred French poodle, Franchot. The failure of the book was bad enough, but Bloodgood's rash had spread to his knees when Leonard Lyons revealed that the whole thing was a hoax, perpetrated by one Paul Niely, a junior at Purdue.

When this story about the book is brought up at the party, Harry Spencer refers to it as *They Ain't Nobody Here but Us Nielys,* and Bloodgood's ankles begin to itch. He is so miserable at the sudden spread of his rash that he doesn't even listen to Spencer's celebrated rendition of the Gettysburg Address in Negro dialect ("All men are cremated eagles," etc.), but this recitation brings John Greenleaf Hanty, formerly of the *Old Masses,* to his feet in scowling but silent rebuke. The Hantys leave, and then the Johnsons, and then the Merrills, and at twelve-thirty Dora Gardner wakes the sleeping Fred and *they* go. Only the Spencers are left. Joan is sitting on the arm of Harry's chair, kissing him on the forehead and coaxing him to do his shaggy-dog story. They had missed the hostess's low and pointed "Heavens, is it *that* late?" when the Gardners left.

Jim Bloodgood decides to let fifteen minutes ride without offering to make another drink, but he doesn't know the Spencers. "Hey!" cries Harry. "How's about the first of a long series of wee doch-an-dorrises?" "That goes double Scotch for me!" laughs Joan. They both clap hands. Bloodgood does not move or say anything, but Laura, with a small sigh worthy of an actress, makes two short ones. "Well, the shorter the quicker," says Harry. "But the larger the sooner," comes back Joan. This is clearly, from their exaggerated laughter, a bit of dialogue they do together at all late parties. They have a stock of small, cryptic family jokes, and they are now reminded of their favorite, a lot of deadpan double-talk about "the honorable cat." After five minutes, this really gets to Jim Bloodgood. He stands up. "I don't know about putting the honorable cat out," he says, "but I got to go to bed. Hard day at the office tomorrow." Laura comes in fast with "Yes, you *must* get to bed, dear. You have *such* a hard day at the office tomorrow."

Let us now observe carefully the effect of this strategy on the Spencers. They exchange winks. Can it be that they have something up their sleeves, something rehearsed for just such a situation as this? "Lie down here, Jim," says Harry, "and we'll throw something over you." The Spencers, side by side, stand in front of the sofa, their glasses raised on high, ready to throw something—but you get it, and so does Bloodgood. "I got to go to bed, goddam it, it's late," he says, itching. "Without a posset?" demands Harry roguishly. He turns to Joan. "Where's the posset?" he asks. "I don't know, sir," says Joan. "I'll see. Here, posset, posset, posset! Here, posset, posset, posset!" She walks around snapping her fingers, until she comes to the bar. "Here's the posset," she says, grabbing up the Scotch bottle. "Give it to me!" snarls Harry, taking the bottle. He pours huge slugs into his glass and Joan's. "That'll teach it a lesson," he says grimly. Jim Bloodgood quickly says good-night, leaves the room, and stamps up the stairs. Laura Bloodgood sinks back in her chair. There is nothing that can save *her*. Not now.

The Spencers suddenly propose a group of toasts: to the late Admiral Sigsbee on his birthday, to Tyler, Rudolph, and James, to the discovery of tungsten in New Mexico, to the honorable cat, and, in mock tears, to the brave men of the sheriff's posset. Harry and Joan are magnificent to-gether when they are buzzed, and they know it. Each appreciates the other's quick ad-libbing, fertile invention, and rich fantasy. They don't need an audience, and they are now practically unaware of their hostess. They just leave her sitting there.

"The first of a series for the road," Harry tosses at Laura Bloodgood in one of his rare, fleeting recognitions of her presence. He has a store of these multiple-nightcap gags, including a wee doch-an-Dora, Dorothy, Dolores, and so on. Laura, stranded in that lonely chair, abandoned by her husband, and getting no help from me, is in for at least two more long and frantic hours. Joan insists that

Harry do his talking-horse routine (the one that takes at least as long as the "Rhapsody in Blue"), but he refuses unless she will do the apache dance with him. So she does.

This is the Spencers' masterpiece and, like almost everything else they do together, it is divided into several parts, and can run from ten minutes after two until a quarter of three. I myself have known the Spencers for a long time, and I can think of no way to break it up now that Bloodgood has gone to bed and plumped the problem in his wife's lap. Harry and Joan interpret the dance as it would be done by a Supreme Court justice and his wife, then by an arthritic psychiatrist and his amorous patient, and finally by a slain dowager and her butler, the slayer. In this finale, which is pretty rough on Joan and the furniture, the weary hostess is forced to take part. She can't get out of it, because the dancers need an assistant for this one, to play the cop. You see, Harry has just shot Joan, and he knows that a policeman (Laura Bloodgood) has heard the shot and is peering through a window. Laura doesn't actually have to go outside the house to peer through a window, but she does have to stand up. She has to stand up and peer for about eleven minutes, the way a cop would, while Harry, with the limp Joan in his arms, dances and dances, to make the cop believe that the dead woman is not only alive but having the time of her life. I have seen this dance some thirty-odd times, and it can be terribly effective, especially when the inert Joan's flying arms and legs manage to knock over everything that isn't built in, during the wild climax of whirls that finally convinces the cop that everything is O.K.

The panting, flushed Spencers at last sit down. Laura collapses. "I think," says Harry, "that calls for a drink." "I'll make it," says Joan to Laura. "You sit where you are."

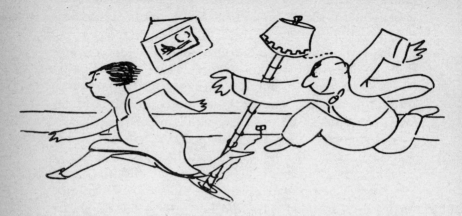

The hostess now begins to talk rapidly, before Harry or Joan can think of some pantomime that requires the throwing of books or the juggling of Spode. She remembers something that Dora Gardner whispered to her over the coffee, about the time Harry tossed Dora's sister-in-law in the air (the one with the weak vertebra) to dramatize some point in one of his acrobatic narratives. Now, right here Mrs. Bloodgood is going to have to be extremely careful—in the topic she selects, I mean. I assume, naturally, that she is smart enough not to mention cats—she must realize the routine *that* will get her back into.

Oh, they go finally, of course, but I am afraid I cannot claim credit for that. The problem is really beyond my powers, much as I would like to solve it on behalf of the Bloodgoods and all the other ladies and gentlemen who are prisoners in their own living rooms whenever the jolly voices of Harry and Joan are heard at the front door.

I have thought of one thing, though. I have thought of a way to get back at the Spencers. I have been asked to dinner at their house next Thursday, and in preparation for the event I have learned by heart "Hiawatha," all the White Sox infields since 1894, a series of thirty-two card tricks, and an interminable *pas seul* that narrates all the major sieges of history from the Bastille to the Alamo. It has wonderful parts in it for Harry and Joan. They have to go upstairs and stay there, to represent the neutral countries.

I know what you're saying. You're saying it won't work. You know what I think? I think you've got something there.

4

Mary Petty and Her Drawings

ᘐᘐᘐᘐᘐᘐᘐᘐᘐᘐᘐᘐᘐᘐᘐᘐᘐᘐᘐᘐᘐᘐᘐᘐᘐᘐᘐᘐᘐᘐᘐᘐᘐᘐᘐᘐᘐᘐ

Mary Petty began to draw for *The New Yorker* eighteen years ago, when she was just a slip of a girl and the magazine was only two years old going on three. It had first ventured upon the crowded and indifferent newsstands in the middle of the great Marathon Phase of American life. Everywhere, men and women were striving to outfly, outswim, outdance, outwalk, outsit, outtalk, outchew, and outrock one another. The loose and gaudy atmosphere of the street fair hung over lane and boulevard. In this curious somatic interlude, the operation of the mind had given way all of a sudden to the exploitation of the body. If it was physical, you had but to name it and the Americans would do it. Human endurance was held up as the highest virtue, and thought became the recourse of oldsters and invalids.

A few writers, who had watched the War for the Preservation of Mankind degenerate into a frivolous and ominous peace, raised cries of warning and disillusionment, but the people did not listen. They were too busy trying to see how long they could hang by their heels or beat on a dishpan with a kitchen spoon. One's progress through the

26

streets was fraught with bizarre dangers. If you stared too long at a man who had been sitting on a flagpole for two months, or gaped incautiously at an airplane that had been circling around and around for ten weeks, you were liable to be knocked down by a gentleman walking backward across the country, or mangled by a car in which a sleepless youth was handcuffed to the steering wheel.

Into the midst of this carnival sauntered the young *New Yorker,* uneasy and a little bewildered, in spite of its jaunty strut and eager eye. The new magazine reflected the reckless detachment of the period. It wore no armor and it sought no grail; it did not carry a sword cane or even an umbrella. Since neither trumpet nor banner had called it into existence, it was not going anywhere to do anything about anything. It was just walking along, like any other visitor from out of town, looking into the expensive store windows, gazing up at the tall buildings, widening its eyes and dropping its jaw at impressive statistics or unusual facts. The amiable periodical tiptoed away from disputes and disturbances, since it had nothing particular in mind to prove or disprove, to attack or defend. Now and then it jostled the celebrated, or thumbed its nose at the powerful, but all in a spirit of gay mockery. *The New Yorker* was not really angry. It just didn't give a good goddam.

At the head of this wildly nonchalant enterprise stood a Borglum figure out of the deep tangled wildwood of the Far West, a brilliant and restless man of distinguished profanity and articulate gesture, who at the tough age of twelve had swung on vines to the quaint little railroad station at Aspen, Colorado, whence he had ridden out into the world to make his fortune. His name was Harold W. Ross.

After a considerable period of wandering about, during which, at one period, he terrorized the neighborhood of the

Place de l'Opéra in the rowdy company of such bully boys as F.P.A. and A. Woollcott, he settled at last in New York where, possibly as the result of a lost wager, he became an associate editor of *Judge*. Quickly bored by the two-line joke, he impetuously borrowed a million dollars from a man he met at a party, and started the brave but aimless magazine whose early days I have so tenderly described.

Although Harold Ross knew, by first name or nickname, all the recognized and exploited talents in town, his magazine was destined to be taken over by a group of unknowns and nobodies. They drifted in from advertising agencies, from cow colleges, from anonymity on other magazines, from obscure jobs on newspapers, and from Paris, where they had not known Fitzgerald or Hemingway or Gertrude Stein.

The newcomers found plenty of room for the lively exercise of their fancies in a publication unhampered by policy or allegiance, whose otherwise disrespectful editor had a high regard for talent and a rare intuitive sense of how to foster its development. As a result, the easy-going *New Yorker* was able to produce in time a number of untrammelled artists with something original to say. A unique member of this little group of nameless talents that popped up out of everywhere and nowhere in the 1920's was Mary Petty, whose drawings for many years have delighted the many, and excited the perspicacious few. This artist, who has woven so large and special a part of *The New Yorker's* bright design, differed from most of the molders of the magazine in that she was a native of New York City. Even so, the editors did not catch sight of her for years. She mailed her drawings in and sedulously avoided the noisy precincts of the publication about which there were so many false and frightening rumors afloat.

The New Yorker was not, in fact, the violent loony bin it had been cracked up to be. Miss Petty would have discovered, in its plain workaday offices, shy and even timorous persons, given to flatulence, tremors, and mild melancholia, and absorbed by family worries and commonplace problems. A group photograph of its editors and resident contributors at that time would have moved the softhearted to send in contributions of food, clothing, money, and inspirational literature.

But Mary Petty would not come near the place, and for a long time nothing at all was known about her—except that she regularly submitted a new and distinctive kind of drawing. Rumors began to circulate that she was a little girl, that she was an old lady, that no such person actually existed. Even later, when it was a fairly common sight to behold her sitting, cool and almost undismayed, on the edge of a chair in the offices she once greatly dreaded, very little was known about her life. The biographer who attempts an extended study of this charming but reticent lady has my sympathy. I can put down in no time at all the few facts I have been permitted to glean. Mary Petty was born in a brownstone house on West End Avenue. Her father was a professor. She did not have a particularly happy childhood. That's all, brother.

About her work she is, under pressure, somewhat more communicative. She never studied art, but taught herself, with the same slow patience and great care with which she makes each of her drawings, sitting in what she insists is a dark corner, surrounded by a ring of eraser crumbs. It takes her three weeks to finish a drawing, and at the end of that time she protests that she hates the drawing and herself. Everybody else, of course, loves it and her.

In her whole career, Mary Petty has done only two drawings from ideas that originated outside her own mind. Many artists depend chiefly on gagmen, and most others profit to a considerable extent from lines sent in to the magazine or suggested by friends. Mary Petty's world, however, is peculiarly, jealously, and devotedly her own. Once in a long while the magazine's busybodies tinker with one of her captions, but these impudent editorial minds (among them, in a moment of lapse, my own) have been completely and properly frustrated in their stubborn attempts to match their pace with hers, to force their way into her incomparable and inviolable houses.

Now that the pieces of Miss Petty's work have been dug out of the files and fitted together into an eloquent whole, it must become clear to the tinkerers that the words of her captions and the lines of her drawings are all of a piece. The Petty idiom and point of view, like the Petty draftsmanship, are intensely original and personal. What this artist has is not a trick, but a magic, and magics are not transferable.

Mary Petty's drawings are always funny, and often uproarious, but now that the carefully selected best have been brought together and we have our first long view of what she has been up to, we can see, beneath the fun, the sharpness of her thrust, the way (to take a line from one of her characters) she hits out at life. In those awful houses her imagination has invaded, she has done a beautiful job on the stuffy, the arrogant, the idle, the complacent, and the empty.

I am fascinated by the revelation in these pages of a device of incongruity which is absolutely her own. She catches time in a foreshortened crouch that intensifies her satirical effects. A lady emerges out of the decorous habiliments of the past and crawls, nude and smirking, into the

30

easy abandon of the present, and you have a sharp new sense of the frailties of both eras. A girl pops out of the 1890's and leaps over a 1945 tennis net into your enchanted but troubled heart. You have the mad feeling that the dowager hoisting her skirts before the mantelpiece is warming herself against the meagre fire of the future. Tomorrow and yesterday and today creeps in "This Petty Pace" from page to page.

But let us leave the business of analysis to the critics, and to the booksy psychiatrists who will weigh the despair, look for the hope, and measure the validity of the affirmation. You and I better just laugh, lest the awesome creep of all periods of our time, suddenly become one, begins to get us.

I commend to all people of courage and sensibility everywhere these penetrating glances into the bright and dark corners of Mary Petty's alarming and hilarious world.

Preface to *This Petty Pace*, 1945

5

Afternoon of a Playwright

ᎯᎯᎯᎯᎯᎯᎯᎯᎯᎯᎯᎯᎯᎯᎯᎯᎯᎯᎯᎯᎯᎯᎯᎯᎯᎯᎯᎯᎯᎯ

I called the other afternoon, at the laudanum hour, upon Bernard Hudley, the dramatist, and found him, to my astonishment, somewhat less despondent than he had been on my previous visit some months before. "What's the matter?" I asked anxiously. "Can I do anything to depress you?"

He didn't answer, but sat staring at a blank piece of paper in his typewriter.

"I am trying to outline a drawing-room comedy of horror," he said finally, "but a note of hope, even of decency, keeps creeping into it."

"That's too bad," I told him. "What's the time of the play? Maybe that's where the fault lies."

He pulled the paper out of the typewriter, tore off a piece, and began chewing it. "It's set in Tanganyika, 600,000 years ago," he said. "I want to show that mankind came to an end that year, and that we do not now, in fact, exist. But 600,000 years ago doesn't seem gloomy enough, somehow."

I thought about his problem for a moment, and then

32

said, "I think I see what's the matter. Why don't you make it 598,000 B.C.?"

His eyes lighted gloomily. "You may have something ghastly there," he admitted.

"But I don't think they had drawing rooms in those years," I told him.

"This is not an ordinary drawing room," he snapped. "I call it a drawing and quartering room."

"Now you're being your old self again," I said. "Who are you using for characters?"

"Devils and demons," he said, "all of them possessed by human beings. I like that part of it all right, but there's nowhere to go from there except up, and you know how I hate up. The first act is terrifying enough to suit me, but I don't know what to do about the second act yet."

I lit the wrong end of a filter cigarette and handed it to him. "What's the scene of the second act?" I asked.

"A combination madhouse and brothel," he said. "A convention of clergymen has taken it over for the weekend. You see what I mean by the note of hope creeping in?"

"I do indeed," I said. I got up, walked to the bar in the corner of the room and picked up a bottle.

"Not that one," he said quickly. "That's poisoned. Take the one on the right." I knew Hudley well enough to figure that the bottle on the right was the poisoned one, so I poured a drink from the one I had selected.

"Damn your intuition!" he snarled. "You're worse than Myra. She has lost her sense of smell completely, but I still can't fool her about those bottles." His wife, Myra, walked into the room at that moment, wearing dark glasses and showing her lower teeth.

"Bad afternoon," I said. "I hope you're feeling awful."

"Bad afternoon," she said, and then to her husband, "It's

time for you not to take your thyroid pills." He didn't say anything.

"You two have been married for three weeks now," I said. "What's the matter?"

"Oh, we have tried everything," she said, "but something always goes right. You know how things are nowadays."

He looked gloomier than ever. "Now Myra's having an affair with a police lieutenant," he told me. "She always picks the wrong man, someone that can't run away with her."

Myra laughed—at least I think it was laughter, although it sounded more like pieces of iron falling into a bathtub. "Bernard wants the girl next door, but she's too old for him," Myra said. "She's nine."

"And not getting any younger, I suppose," I put in, unable to think of anything else.

Suddenly, from somewhere in the house, there were two pistol shots in rapid succession.

"This house is the noisiest place this side of hell," growled Hudley.

"Who's shooting who?" I asked as casually as I could.

Myra took a drink straight from the bottle from which I had poured mine. "Either my sister has shot her lover, or vice versa," she said.

"Well, don't go and find out," her husband croaked. "I've no time for details. Maybe I ought to go back to that play about the Wright brothers at Kitty Hawk."

"Why did you drop it in the first place?" I asked him.

"It got cheerful on me," he said. "I call them the Fright brothers and made the setting Night Hawk. They both crack up on their first flight, and that prevents the development of the airplane."

"I see," I said. "It *is* cheerful. That would, of course,

34

have prevented the invention of the modern bomber and all the other deadly warplanes."

Myra sat down in a chair and began reading a copy of a magazine called *Horrible Love Tales*. I began to feel, for some reason, a little nervous. "What became of the play you were working on last year called *The Explosion*?" I asked.

"Couldn't find a producer," Hudley grumbled. "They all said it needed development, that it was too short."

"What did they mean?" I asked.

Hudley ate another piece of paper, and said, "The curtain goes up on an empty stage, and before any character appears the whole damn set blows up. It seemed gruesome enough to me, and definitely unique."

Myra gave her iron laugh again. "Gruesome, hell!" she said. "Most hilarious play he ever wrote. You don't see anybody get killed, and, furthermore, the audience could leave the theatre and go to the nearest bar and have a good time."

"There ought to be a law against people having a good time," I said, and stood up. "Bad by." I bowed to both of them, and backed out of the room toward the front door, so that I wouldn't be stabbed or shot in the back.

As I went down the front steps of the Hudley house, a man in the uniform of a police lieutenant came up to me. It was Myra's lover. "Somebody reported hearing shots in there," he said, and added, hopefully, "Did she get Hudley this time?"

"No," I told him. "Mrs. Hudley's sister shot her lover, or he shot her. We were pretty busy discussing modern plays and nobody had time to look."

"You better come back with me, Mac," he said. "Maybe I can pin it on you. I love to pin crimes on the wrong man."

"You ought to be a playwright," I told him. "You seem to have a natural talent for the modern drama."

He led me back into the house and, when we got to the living room, both Hudley and Myra were lying on the floor. They had bored each other to death in my absence.

"Always business." The lieutenant laughed horribly. "I never have a cheerless moment." He went to the telephone and called the police station. "Let me have Police Inspector Rawlings," he said, and then, "What do you mean, he isn't there? Gone out of town? How long will he be gone? Two days? Good."

"You said good," I told him. "That's bad."

"We all make mistakes," he snarled, and he dialed another number. "Is this Inspector Rawlings' house?" he said into the receiver. "Let me talk to Mrs. Rawlings." There was a pause, and then he said, "Eleanor? I've just found out your husband is out of town for two days. Put on something uncomfortable. I'll be right over." He hung up and started out of the room. As he stepped over what I had thought was Hudley's dead body, the playwright deftly tripped him, causing him to fall and break his neck.

"Somebody will have to call Mrs. Rawlings," I said, and Myra sat up, with the eager look of a little girl at a circus. "I'll handle that," she said brightly, as she went to the phone.

36

"I think I know what to do with the clergymen in the brothel," I told Hudley.

"It better be awful," he snarled.

"It is," I said. "Why not make them all insane? Then you could call the play *Too Many Kooks Spoil the Brothel*."

Hudley and Myra pulled guns on me at the same moment, but before they could fire their little son walked into the room and got both of them with a double-barrelled shotgun. "Dad wouldn't let me have the car tonight," he explained. "And Mom wanted me to do my homework." Suddenly he drew a knife and threw it at me.

"Wake up! Wake up!" said my wife's voice, from the next bed. I woke up groggily.

"What became of all the bodies?" I mumbled.

"I don't know and I don't care," my wife said, "but you were yelling in your sleep. Don't you *ever* have any pleasant dreams?" I glanced at my wristwatch. It was a quarter after six. I didn't know whether to get up, or try to go back to sleep. It was nightmare either way.

"You want a drink?" I asked my wife, but she was asleep again. I dressed and went downstairs, and poured myself a stiff drink of straight whiskey. I raised the glass and said to the vanished figures of my nightmare, "There's no place to go but down." Then I downed the drink. An hour later I was feeling much worse. I had picked the wrong bottle, the unpoisoned one.

6

The Other Room

ᚢᚢᚢᚢᚢᚢᚢᚢᚢᚢᚢᚢᚢᚢᚢᚢᚢᚢᚢᚢᚢ

The bar of the Hôtel Continental in Paris is large and comfortable, and never too crowded, especially in October, when the American invaders are beginning to thin out, and it is presided over by an efficient and amiable waiter named Jacques. He had just brought drinks for my wife and me and an English painter we know. You can lean back in the Continental bar, drinking for pleasure, slowly, in the European manner, without the urge to see how soon you can reach the point when you no longer know you're drinking, in the American manner.

An American woman, at a near-by table, was explaining to a friend the reason for her dermatitis, insisting that it had been caused by aluminum pots and pans.

"My allergist says I have an emotional conflict or something," she said. "Doctors always say there's something the matter with you, but it's almost always something you use around the house, or wear, or eat. Of course, I'm terribly high-strung, I know that," she said, "but it isn't that. If it was I'd know it."

The Continental bar, like any other place where Americans gather, is used largely for the exchange of symptoms,

38

complaints about French coffee, and the enumeration of hotels and restaurants on the Continent and in England which one should, at all costs, avoid.

We were waiting for three persons to join us, all of them compatriots of ours—one a twenty-two-year-old American girl, the daughter of friends of ours back home, and the other two a man and his wife, friends of friends of ours, neither of whom we had ever met. We had got, a few days before, the usual note from somebody in New York, saying that she had instructed the Barretts to look us up at the hotel, and, in the unfailing routine of such matters, they had telephoned and we had made a date for drinks, hoping they would not recite too many symptoms or complaints before we could get rid of them.

The painter was telling us about his own favorite hotel, a mythical composite one, invented in the imagination of a friend of his, and called the Hôtel Pas-de-Calais-et-Pas-de-Confort, when a nine-year-old girl, unmistakably American, and loose momentarily from her parents, materialized at my elbow. She had dashed into the bar to look at the television set near the door leading into the dining room.

"It's in French," she said. "It ought to be in English. Why isn't it in English?" I explained to her that it was not in English in the same way that television in America was not in French, but she was unconvinced and clearly unimpressed by my knowledge of such things. The small interruption annoyed me, because I had been on the point of describing my own favorite French hostelry, the Hôtel-de-l'Univers-et-de-Massachusetts.

"Tell me a story," commanded the little girl. "My name is Eunice." She squirmed into a chair and stared at me.

"Well, did you ever hear of the Teapot Dome scandal?" I asked.

"I don't think I like it," she said. "What is it?"

"You surely know what a teapot dome is," I said. She got up, frowning, stood on her toes a moment, and sat down again. "Yes," she said.

I began to drink faster, in the American manner, and said, "A scandal is when a teapot dome doesn't obey its parents, but runs in and out of bars, and won't eat anything for bekkus except lint and buttons. Well, this particular teapot dome was—"

A large woman, obviously the child's mother, loomed up suddenly out of nowhere, like a pirate ship. "We never say bekkus to Eunice," she said. "She loathes it."

"I loathe it," said Eunice.

"Sorry," I said. "It has been so long since I was a little girl I have forgotten."

"Now, now," said my wife. "You were going to be nice this evening."

"For a change," our painter friend asked, "or just as a noble experiment?"

"Well!" said the ignored mother, and she dragged the little girl away.

"What happened to the Teapot Dome scandal? You can't just leave it hanging there, you know," said the painter, but I left it hanging there, for my wife said, "Here's Linda now."

Linda Gray, fresh-looking and pretty, with the eyes of an angel, said she was sorry she was late, but I reminded her that American girls were always late, and she was introduced to our English friend.

"Mr. Middleton would like to paint you, I am sure," I said.

"I am a gifted man," Middleton said, "but not that gifted. The portrait of this lady would require something more ethereal than paint."

My wife asked Linda what she would like to drink, and she asked for a Coca-Cola. "I have had an adventure," she said. "Not a very pleasant one."

"I hope it isn't too racy," I said. "My wife has led a cloistered life, and believes that the storks find babies under cabbage leaves."

"Oh, it wasn't like that," Linda said, with a slight *frisson*. "I had just turned away from the window of a shop on the Rue de Rivoli when this American—he must have been about sixty—spoke to me. It's terrible, or sad, or something, but it's usually an American, a middle-aged American, who speaks to us girls on the street, not a Frenchman or any other foreigner."

"What did he say?" my wife wanted to know. Linda paused a moment. "He said '*Combien pour toute la nuit?*' " she said.

"He *must* be at least sixty," I said. "That goes back to the battle of Paris in the First World War. I know all the verses."

"You would," my wife said.

"I used to sing them with the fellows," I said, "but I never said them to the girls."

"I just looked at him," Linda said, "and told him, 'I am an American girl.' I really put my best Sunday virtue into it. Funny, he seemed to look at me and past me too. It was odd, and gave me the shivers a little. Then he said something I didn't understand and walked away."

"Travel is broadening, but disillusioning," said Middleton.

"I know the type," I said, "for I make a study of morbid things. He probably hadn't made a pass at a woman for twenty years back home. Over here, on summer holiday, they get away from their wives, who are out shopping, and

41

the devil takes hold of them. He was probably just trying to recapture his lost youth. Paris has a strange effect on the middle-aged American male, something like the loss of inhibition that takes place on shipboard. Of course, it happens to the American woman, too, sometimes. I knew a cruise director, once, who told me that he had had affairs with women on ships who wouldn't have spoken to him on land."

"Human nature, as Montaigne or somebody said years ago, is capable of curious behavior," Middleton put in. "The dark unfathomed caves of notion, to coin a phrase—a rather pretty phrase, if I may say so."

"My God, there he is now!" said Linda. The man she was looking at had just come into the bar and begun looking around. He was sixty, all right, with a familiar harried look, and the sagging shoulders of a man who has sat for years at a desk.

"I hope it isn't Barrett," my wife said, but it was Barrett. He headed straight for our table, walking with a slight limp.

"In the midst of life we are in *worse* than death," Middleton said.

"I'd better go," Linda said. "I'd better go."

"He won't remember you," I told her. "Don't recognize him."

"If he could forget this girl's eyes," Middleton said, "he is something less than normal."

I said, "Are you Mr. Barrett?" before he could say anything, but managed to keep both hands busy, one holding my drink, the other my cigarette. I didn't know what to say, but I had to say something.

"You been behaving yourself, Mr. Barrett?" I asked.

"Have to," he said. "Got the little woman with me, you

know." We managed the introduction somehow. Barrett recognized Linda, there was no doubt about that. He was for three seconds a statue in bronze, a frightened statue, a little tired, a little older than the man who had walked into the room. My wife did her best to cover it over with roses, asking where Mrs. Barrett was, and how she was, and how long they were going to stay, and how our mutual friends in New York were, trying to bring some ease to the bronze figure of a trapped, middle-aged, middle-class American man, whose lack of social resource was as evident as wind on a prairie.

Jacques appeared, and more drinks were ordered, and the ease that Jacques invariably brings to a table of Americans helped a little to break the tableau and the spell.

"I'll have a Scotch and soda, this time," Linda said.

"Do that twice," Barrett said, and it seemed to me I had known he was going to say just that. Middleton sat studying us all as if he were about to sketch in a composition, a conversation piece.

Barrett sat down stiffly and uneasily on the edge of a chair, the unhappiest man I had seen that summer—or any other summer, for that matter. I felt enormously sorry for him.

"Were you in the First World War, the war the French still call '*La Grande Guerre*'?" I asked, and he sat back a little and came as close as he could to relaxing.

"I was there, Charley," he said, almost as if to himself. "This is the first time I have seen Paris since those days. I was at Fère-en-Tardenois, and I got shoved around up there. It was pretty rough going."

"Never rougher anywhere," I agreed. "I knew two guys who were there," and I told him their names, but I don't think he was listening. "Yeah, sure, yeah, sure," he said.

"The Heinies knocked off a lot of us. It was like fighting in a room. They were on all sides of you. I drove out there the other day, hired a car and drove out there. As I got closer to the battlefield, I got scared, I don't mind saying. I wanted to tell the guy to turn around and drive back to Paris, but I didn't. We came to this sign that says 'Fère-en-Tardenois—14 km.'; and it seemed like two hours from there. There's a big American cemetery there now." He was glad to get the Scotch he had ordered, but his hand shook when he picked it up.

"One of the men I knew was made a sergeant on the field," I said. "All the sergeants of his company had been killed. He got out of it alive, but he carried shrapnel with him all his life, and was in and out of hospitals."

"Yeah, sure," said Barrett. "I got some stuff in me, too. I got a silver plate, I got two silver plates." He touched his right leg and then the left side of his head. "It seems to me I was always in hospitals, army hospitals, in my twenties." He gave a troubled sigh. "What I seem to remember most is hospitals. When I get nightmares, even my office turns into a hospital, even now."

There was a softening of the tension in the air, a little, I thought, like candlelight replacing the glare of torches. Nobody said anything for a moment except Linda. "I'm sorry," Linda said.

"Where is Mrs. Barrett?" my wife asked, tactfully shifting gears.

"I don't know," Barrett said. "I was to meet her here. She's always on time, she's always ahead of me."

"Perhaps she left a message for you at the desk," my wife said. "Shall I find out?"

Barrett stood up, saying, "No, no, I'll go out and ask," and he went out of the bar.

44

"He's kind of nice," said Linda, after a long moment. "He has a nice smile. I wish he had smiled when he spoke to me on the street, but he didn't."

"I think he needs another drink," I said. Barrett had finished his drink fast, as nervous men do, and so I signalled Jacques. "The same again, all around," I told him.

"I don't know anything about him or his wife," my wife put in. "All that Ella said in her note was something about 'Please be nice to the Barretts. They have both been through a lot. I'll tell you about it later.' Ella signed the letter 'Hastily.' Everybody is always in such a rush."

"You never know what the boys who survived Fère-en-Tardenois are going to say or do," I said, "or how much they are going to drink. You've either been through a battle like that, or you haven't."

"I don't think he should have driven up there," Linda said. "I don't think it was good for him."

"I do," Middleton said. "Maybe he'll get it out of his nightmares, now. Maybe his office will turn into an office again in his dreams."

Barrett came back to the table, looking even more tired, and somehow grayer. "Martha is lying down," he told us. "This trip has pretty well tuckered her out. We shouldn't have done that châteaux tour, I guess. It took a lot out of her." He didn't sit down. "Well, thank you for the drink," he said. "It was nice of you to ask us."

"You're not going yet," I told him. "We've ordered you another drink." His face brightened a little and, after a slight pause, he sat down again, this time farther back in his chair.

"Tell us some more about the war," I said. "Maybe it will get those hospitals out of your nightmares." He gave us his slow, gentle smile. "It wasn't so much the battle, or even hospitals," he began, finally. "At least, that's what one of the docs in the States told me back in the twenties. It was something that happened in the battle of Paris, I guess. Anyway, this doc said so." The new drinks arrived, and he picked his up eagerly.

"What was it?" Linda asked.

"Kind of a silly thing, it was," he said. "We come from Iowa, you know, Cedar Rapids. I was only twenty-one when I got to France, and I thought it was a million miles from anywhere. You get homesick when you're that young, and are that far away from home. It's worse than the battle. You get through the battle somehow, and you don't think much about it till later in the hospital, or when you fall asleep. They had given me a lot of stuff to make me sleep, and I'd never taken dope before." He drank some more of his whiskey and soda. "I remember Paris clearer than anything," he said, "but I can't remember how I got here, or just when it was. I got out of the base hospital, because I couldn't take it any longer, and I got to Paris. I was AWOL. It's all pretty hazy."

After this confession, he sat for a long time without saying anything, and we waited.

"I remember walking along the Champs-Elysées," he began finally. "I never could pronounce it right." He was correct about that, but none of us pronounced the words for him. "Then, there was this girl, this French girl. She wasn't any older than I was. She spoke English, though, and was I glad for that! Well, we sat out in front of the Café de la Paix. We drove there in a taxi. She said she thought I didn't look very well, and she said she thought I should have something to drink. And so we had a couple of drinks. Then she told me about herself. She came from some place in Southern France, and her father was a drunkard, and

46

used to beat up the family on Saturday nights, so she ran away to Paris, and got some work in a garment factory, but all they gave her was a few francs a week, and she saw all these other girls in fur coats and things, and so she took to—well, making the boys feel better, she called it." This time, there was an even longer silence, but we all waited politely and attentively.

"I never told Martha about all this," he took up again. "But the other day I took a taxi up to the street where this French girl used to have an apartment. I remembered the street, and even the number, I remembered the number, too. They call it Rue Marcadet, and it's up there in Montmartre. I didn't get out of the cab. Maybe I should have, but I didn't get out. I just looked at the building, the windows on the second floor. Nobody there would know about her now. Her name was Françoise, but she told me to call her Frances, and so I called her Frances. She would be sixty now. Doesn't seem possible, but she would be sixty now. Well, like I said, she was only twenty herself then, but there were pictures of guys all over her living room,

47

guys in uniform, guys of all the allied countries. The picture I can't forget was a picture of a young Canadian soldier. She had it framed, and it was sitting on her piano. He was a handsome fella, and he couldn't have been more than twenty himself." He looked at Linda, as if she were too young to hear the rest of the story, but she said, "I'm much older than any of you were. I'm twenty-two."

"Well, of course, I never saw the Canadian boy, but he gets into my dreams, too, kinda banged up, with his uniform all bloody. You see, she found out from a buddy of his later that he had been killed in action. This friend of his brought her this note he had written her, the last note he had ever written, I guess. She showed it to me one day in her apartment—the first and only time I ever went there," he added hastily. "I remember what it said, all right, every word of it, though I don't remember things as well as I used to." He took some more of his drink and set the glass on the table.

"Finish that," I told him, "and we'll get another one."

"No, no," he said, with his little smile, "I never have more than two. Well, she had a bottle of port wine at her place, and we sat there drinking this port wine, too much of it, I guess. After a while, she went out of the room into—the other room, and left me sitting there with the whole damn war all around me, it seemed like. This good-looking boy on the piano kept staring at me, and looking sad, and awful young—like that part from 'St. James Infirmary.'"

"'So young, so cold, so fair,'" Linda murmured.

"Yeah, that's it," Barrett said. He picked up his glass again, and leaned back in his chair, and sighed deeply. "Well, I sat there, thinking of too many things, thinking of everything, the way it all floods back on you, you know." We all nodded together. "I thought of a girl back home in Iowa, who was only seventeen then, I thought of Martha.

Then I heard this French girl calling to me from—the other room." He sat forward again, and seemed to stiffen, and his voice, when he spoke again, seemed very far away. "Well, I got up and left the place. I guess I kinda ran out on her. It wasn't until I got into the street that I realized I was carrying my glass, and it still had some port wine in it. I put it down somewhere, and went on walking. I must've walked for miles. The next thing I really remember I was back at the hospital. I guess the MP's got me."

He broke off his recital to finish his drink, and then he stood up. "After that, for a while, I went into a nose dive, kinda what the docs call nervous prostitution," he (and Sigmund Freud) said. None of us laughed, or even smiled. "There were a lot of songs we all sang in those days," he said, "some of them, well, kinda naughty, as the ladies say. I was thinking of them today, walking around Paris, I was thinking about a lot of things. Seemed like it was 1918 again, and I was young and back in Paris." He picked up his glass from the table and drained the last drop, and set it down again. "This girl, this Frances, gets in my dreams sometimes too. But the door is always locked, or something, or the floor to the other room is gone, like it was blown away."

"All doors open sooner or later. Maybe this one will now," I said, trying to be cheerful.

"Well," Barrett said, "you've all been very nice to me today, and I appreciate it, and I know Martha will, too. I wish you could meet Martha. She's very sweet. I don't know what I would have done without Martha. She's got me through a lot of things."

"Oh, we'll see you again," my wife said, "and Martha, too. Tell her I'll send her some flowers. How long are you going to be here?"

"Three days," Barrett said, "three days, and then we're sailing back on the *Liberté*. I like the French ships, I like France."

Linda suddenly stood up, and ran, rather than walked, around the table. She was tall, in the manner of American girls of today, almost as tall as Barrett, so she did not have to stand on tiptoe when she kissed him on the forehead. "I like you, too," she said, warmly. "I think you're lovely." He patted her hand twice, and then said something none of us could understand, and hurriedly walked away.

"I'm sixty years old myself," I said, "but mighty spry for a man that age, and I'll be even spryer if we have another drink."

"I should say we all need what you Americans call a flock of drinks," Middleton said. My wife called Jacques.

Before we left the Continental bar, all of us except Middleton had reached the point where we weren't quite sure we were still drinking. At that point, I have an inveterate tendency to sing, and my wife sensed this moment had come. "Not here in the bar," she said. "You can sing in the cab on the way to the Chope Danton." In the cab, I said, "How about 'It's a Long Long Way to Tipperary,' or 'Where a Nightingale Is Singing and a Pale Moon Beams'?"

"Not that, not one of *them*," Linda said. "I want to hear '*Combien pour Toute la Nuit?*'" And so I sang for her, in fair voice, and on key for once in my life, "*Combien pour Toute la Nuit?*"

7

The Lady from the Land

∿∿∿∿∿∿∿∿∿∿∿∿∿∿∿∿∿∿∿∿∿∿∿∿∿∿∿∿∿∿∿∿∿∿

A recent hostess of mine, who gave an Anglo-American cocktail party for forty persons (at which the customary seventy showed up), had selected for the moist event one of the large rooms on the first floor of a famous London hotel. It was fun, that party, until the woman I shall call the Lady from the Land sat down beside me. Something told me that I was going to be reproved or reproached or upbraided or rebuffed, and something was right. What she had to say, or rather to reiterate, was a complaint about a piece I wrote for *Punch* last year in which I predicted that, if our species didn't look up and behave, the porpoises would come in from the sea and replace us as the chief mammal on earth.

"I don't think God likes you for that," the lady said. "She doesn't like people who deride, or degrade, the human species."

"She?" I asked.

"I've always believed that God is feminine," she told me. "As a Woman, She would naturally be interested in

51

Mankind, and would never allow the tortoises to take over, as you call it."

I choked slightly on the fresh Scotch and soda the waiter had just handed me. "I did not say tortoises, madam," I told her. "I said porpoises."

She waved this away with an impatient gesture. "It's the same thing," she said.

I lit a cigarette and recited "Listen, my children, and you shall hear of the midnight ride of Paula Revere."

Our hostess suddenly appeared, carrying a martini, and said to me, in what she intended to be a whisper, "Don't be profound." I knew then that the martini was her fourth, and I said to her, "The girl stood on the burning deck whence all but she had fled." My hostess fled, but my critic didn't.

"All that you men care about is the sea," my companion said. "You hear voices from the sea. I've been doing some research on it, and I know. In *Juno and the Paycock* the Paycock says 'The sea is callin' me.' Tennyson wrote, 'One clear call for me, and may there be no moaning of the bar when I put out to sea.'"

"May I—" I began.

"Hear me out," she said. She took a drink from the waiter's tray and I took two, as she went on talking. "Robert Adlai Stevenson said—"

"Louis," I corrected her.

"Don't be rude!" she said. "I'm no loonier than you are. Stevenson said 'Home is the sailor, home from sea.' You men often have to be drafted for war, but you run away to sea. You can hardly wait."

During her lecture I had kept hearing slight hiccups, and realized that a gentleman guest with several sails in the wind had been listening. "Let's get it right," he said.

52

"Stevenson didn't want to be buried at sea. He wrote 'Under the wide and starry sky, dig the grave and let me lie. This be the verse you grave for me: here he lies where he longed to be, and he laid him down with a will.' "

The intruder began laughing loudly, as he managed to get out of his chair. "If he laid him down with a will, then he died intestate," he chortled, and he went reeling away to tell it to somebody else.

"I hate the word 'intestate,' " my companion said. "Why do they have to give old men's diseases such awful names?"

"You are thinking of intestatitis, madam," I said coldly. "Intestate means he died without a will."

"But that man said he died *with* a will," she said sharply.

I was on the point, I'm afraid, of saying, "Ah, shut up!" but saved myself just in time, and began on my second drink of the two new ones. She kept right on bickering.

"Your Eugene O'Neill in *Anna Christie* goes on and on about that old devil sea."

"Davil," I corrected her, but she said, "Quibble, quibble." This time I made her hear *me* out. "What are you working up to, madam, or away from, may I ask?"

"I'm working up to that silly play by Hendrik Hudson," she said. "I mean *The Lady from the Sea*." I decided to let her make a playwright out of Hendrik Hudson, and just went on drinking. "Now then, no woman hears the call of the sea. It's just you men. You're all Joseph Conrads and William McFees at heart. I think it's perfectly dreadful that your poet Longfellow, when he wrote about the schooner *Hesperus,* said, 'The skipper had brought his little daughter to bear him company.' Where was the child's mother all that time?"

"It's an old tradition of the sea that a woman aboard a ship is unlucky," I told her, "and it has always turned

53

out that way. You may not know it, but the skipper's wife was aboard the mystery ship, the *Mary Celeste,* which should have been called the *Harry Celeste,* and then nothing would have happened to it."

"That's right, that's right!" my companion exclaimed. "Blame everything on us women. You even call your ships 'she' so that you can blame it on us when they go down or disappear."

"If you are writing a monograph about all this," I said, "you are wasting your valuable time substituting Scotch for ink."

I was about to get up and join some people, half of whom were taking Kenneth Tynan apart while the other half kept putting him back together again, when another male guest loomed up in front of me. He held an unlighted cigarette in one hand and a matchbox in the other. "I've given up smoking," he said. "Nobody could make me smoke again, not even my wife when I'm mad at her." He broke the cigarette in two and tossed it away, and brought out another one, which he put in his mouth. "You couldn't make me smoke this cigarette, even at gunpoint," he proclaimed loudly.

I pointed my right index finger at him as if it were a gun barrel and said, "We'll see about that. Now then, either you smoke that cigarette, sir, or I shall pull the trigger."

He paused a moment, then lit the cigarette and inhaled deeply. "You made me smoke," he snarled. "Remember that." And he walked away, inhaling.

This time I took three Scotches from the waiter's tray, put one on the floor near me, and held the other two in my hands. Suddenly another woman was in the chair beside me. She took the highball from my left hand.

"I hear you're crazy about the sea," she said.

"Crazy is correct," I told her. "And it's the only accurate thing I've heard said this evening."

Her voice became brighter. "Is it true," she demanded, "that if a ship is sinking from too much cargo, they throw the supercargo overboard?"

"That's a lot of jetsam, madam," I told her. "They don't have to throw him overboard. He jumps. The sea is calling him."

At this point my wife appeared, for we had a dinner date. I heard my new companion whisper to her, in a worried tone, "Your husband thinks that a ship's cargo is human." And she went away.

"I think we'd better leave now," my wife said, and I stood up, on a fairly even keel.

"The proper maritime term is shove off," I told her.

"Why in the world have you been going on about the

sea to everybody?" my wife demanded. "I hope you'll be all right at dinner," she added anxiously.

As we started out, the Lady from the Land sailed up to us. I finished the drink I was still carrying, and turned upon her. "Don't kiss me, Mrs. Hardy," I said brusquely.

My wife took my arm and dragged me away, leaving the Lady standing there speechless for once in her life.

"I simply have to have another drink at the bar," I told my wife on the way out of the hotel, and we went into the bar. This time I had a straight Scotch, and was beginning to relax when my wife abruptly said, "I can't understand why they have to keep weighing the anchor on a ship all the time. It's made of iron, and I don't see how its weight could possibly change." I thought that over for a moment, but didn't say anything, because the bartender was listening intently. After all, I do not want to be committed to a mental institution during this visit of mine to the Port of London.

"Down the hatch!" I said, and we finished our drinks and shoved off.

"That woman you called Mrs. Hardy is a brilliant writer," my wife remarked. "Didn't you know that?"

"Brilliant, but listing heavily—listing heavily to Scotch," I said. "She believes that Ibsen discovered the Hudson River. Nobody gets anything right any more. Mrs. Hardy goes around telling everybody that I believe the tortoises are going to take over."

My wife laughed merrily, and then said, "To-morrow and to-morrow and to-morrow creeps in this carapace from day to day."

I knew I couldn't top that, so I went on with her to the dinner party in sulky silence.

8

Return of the Native

ᖇᖇᖇᖇᖇᖇᖇᖇᖇᖇᖇᖇᖇᖇᖇᖇᖇᖇᖇᖇᖇᖇᖇᖇᖇ

I went back to Ohio last year, to the town where I was born in the middle of the tranquil old decade that considered itself such a devil, the 1890's, with its flamboyant Teddy Roosevelt and its gaudy Oscar Wilde, the diavolos, the wood-burning sets, the euchre and pedro parties, the leather cushions with Indian heads on them, the noisy bamboo portieres, the Turkish corners in living rooms, the pug dogs, the brightly enamelled bicycles, the books of Stanley Weyman and Owen Meredith, and such daring songs as "After the Ball," "Gypsy Love Song," and "Down Where the Wurzburger Flows."

I was just six at the turn of the century, but I remember the Columbus, Ohio, of those somnolent years as fondly and sharply as a man on a sinking ship might remember his prairie home and its dangers no greater than gopher holes or poison ivy. In 1900, Columbus hadn't had a serious threat to its repose since Morgan's Confederate raiders insolently approached the city during the Civil War. There was a lot of picnicking and canoeing and cycling, and going for hikes in the woods on Sundays in spring, the men in boaters and bright blazers, and the women in shirtwaists

57

and skirts. The men got up baseball games, and the women looked for white violets and maidenhair ferns to take home and transplant. People liked to sit on the wide verandas on the hotter Sundays, the men with their feet up on the balustrades, reading in the sports pages about Corbett and Jeffries, Maud S and Star Pointer, Cy Young and John McGraw. The women sat more decorously, reading *The Lady of Lyons* or *Lucile,* and the children, sprawled on the floor, eagerly followed the comic adventures of the Katzenjammer Kids, Lulu and Leander, Happy Hooligan,

Foxy Grandpa, Buster Brown, and Alphonse and Gaston. A couple of young men named Orville and Wilbur were thinking about the laws governing the sustained flight of heavier-than-air contraptions, but people were more interested in the cakewalk than in the gas engine. Columbus and the world can never recapture the serene spirit of those years. This is known as Progress.

Columbus has grown in the last fifty years, in area, in population, and in pride, but many of the houses I once lived in have changed very little. I think I could get around in them in the dark, remembering the halls and the rooms—in all of them, that is, except my grandfather's. It has become a duplex now, and Bryden Road, on which it stands, has lost its old arrogance. There used to be a bold wrought-iron sign, high above the street, bearing the words "Bryden Road" in gilt letters, and the megaphone men on sightseeing buses, which are things of the past, used to bellow at the passengers, "You are now on Bryden Road, the pride of Columbus." Sitting on my grandfather's porch, in the early years of automobiles, my brothers and I used to pick out the Thomas Flyers, the Ramblers, the Loziers, and the Pope-Toledos.

It must have been in 1909 that Columbus constructed a hundred arches over High Street, each of them containing a hundred electric light bulbs. This was considered a handsome and inspiring spectacle at night, and the city council voted to call Columbus "The Arch City." Ceremonies were held, and a telegram of congratulations from Thomas A. Edison was read. A few years later the arches were quietly taken down. By that time, a mayor of Columbus, named George Karb, had dubbed the city "good old Columbus town," and it is still called that in the newspapers—and by visitors or returning natives, if they know what is good for them.

Columbus is proud of its water supply system, its clean city government—as a reporter many years ago, I was once called in to witness a city official rejecting a bribe of ten thousand dollars—and a number of its sons and daughters. These include Elsie Janis, W. E. Burnett, who wrote *Little Caesar*, Dorothy Canfield Fisher, whose father was once president of Ohio State University, Donald Ogden Stewart, Eddie Rickenbacker, Hank Gowdy, hero of the 1914 World Series, and last and greatest, Charles W. (Chic) Harley, whose dazzling feats on the gridiron from 1916 to 1919 are as fresh in the memory of every Columbus resident as they were more than thirty years ago.

When Chic Harley returns to Columbus, the papers run headlines like this: "The Only One Comes Back Home." A few years ago, a sports writer from New York was surprised to learn that the words "he" and "him," if used without a name, always refer to Harley. I had warned my wife about this the first time I took her to Columbus, and she was able to hold her own when a man I had just introduced suddenly said, "I can see him now, out there on the field." Harley had a way of winning games in the last minute of play. Once, he had to kick a goal after a touchdown to win a game by one point. The field was muddy. He asked permission to change his right shoe. Thousands of people held their breath as he calmly did so. Then he sauntered back and casually kicked the goal.

A few years ago I received from a friend still in Columbus two clippings of news events in Columbus. One told of an aged minister who killed his wife because, as he explained to the police, "her number came up." He showed them the number, too. It was the manufacturer's number on the kitchen range—B 17863344. My own number, I have sometimes feared, is much simpler than that, something like 172. The other clipping told of an elderly woman who had shot and wounded a truant officer. The man had come to her kitchen door to find out why her granddaughter was not in school and the woman said, "Wait a minute" and got her gun. "I just pulled the trigger and let 'er go," she explained to the police.

My friend had typed out only one line in the note that accompanied the clippings. It read, "Why don't you come back to Ohio, where no news is practically the only good news?" I went back to Ohio again last year, but it wasn't quite the same, and never will be again.

9

The Danger in the House

ͽͽͽͽͽͽͽͽͽͽͽͽͽͽͽͽͽͽͽͽͽͽͽͽͽ

Dr. Morton Prell and I are on the faculty of a Connecticut university, live not far apart in the college town, and see a great deal of each other. My name is George Merry, which has, in relation to this present report, a small and special significance, as we shall see. Morton teaches psychology and is older than I am in years, but often younger, it seems to me, in debate.

The other night, in my library after dinner, we took up again what has become this winter's postprandial discussion. Dr. Prell has said, testily, and, I think, unfairly, that I have given up discussion for oration. However that may be, our evening explorations of unconscious symbolism, both universal and unique, have not been, at least when I am allowed to talk, unrewarding. My own field is English literature, and Dr. Prell regards me as an amateur in psychology, but then his judgments are sometimes tinged with a curious envy.

The other night we began, over a second brandy, with my recital of a dream I had had when I was six, in 1921. Dr. Prell dismissed this memory as a piece of putative dialectical paramnesia, if I understood him correctly, and I'm pretty sure I didn't. He frequently uses defensive obfuscation on me when I have him backed into a polemical corner. Our wives were in the living room, where, in my house or his, they sometimes seek to find the latent meaning of some of our behavior, such as his habit of lighting his spectacles instead of his cigar, and my occasional search for a belt or necktie which I am either wearing at the time or holding in my hand. The ladies are, to be candid about it, non-intellectuals given to distressing, and often headlong oversimplifications.

On the night of our most recent discussion, I told Dr. Prell a remarkable narrative dream of mine that had a truly O. Henryesque ending. The dream had two settings: the first a room with a low, raftered ceiling. In it, besides myself, were two silent, motionless figures—a man in uniform whose right arm was missing, and a woman in a long white dress who held in her right hand something that glittered, an extraordinarily complicated piece of mechanism. At this point Dr. Prell interrupted by asking if the mechanism may not have *been* her hand instead of *in* it, after which he quoted from T. S. Eliot:

> When lovely woman stoops to folly
> And finds herself again alone,
> She combs her hair with automatic hand
> And puts a record on the gramophone.

He wanted to know if any lovely woman had ever threatened to shoot me. My colleague is, alas, a Longfellow lover whose knowledge of modern poetry, outside of "The Wasteland," is scanty at best. I ignored his irrelevant quotation and went on with my story. "I had a sense of great uneasiness in this dream, a feeling that there was a danger in

63

the house," I said. "Of course, you will say that the man, because of his uniform and missing right arm, represented some colleague of mine whom I fear and envy because he can do better work than I can with one arm tied behind him."

"Don't tell me what I will say," Dr. Prell said sharply. "Get on with it."

"Suddenly the scene shifted," I went on. "I was in a bedroom, apparently on the second floor of the house. Through the open door I could see two other doors across the hall. The man went into one of these rooms and I heard him lock and bolt his door. Then the woman went into the other room and I heard her lock and bolt her door. Oh, Prell, you're about to light your spectacles again. Your cigar is in the ashtray."

"Thank you," said Dr. Prell coldly, and he managed to put the spectacles and the cigar where they belonged. "Your delusion that I am forever about to light my glasses is based on an unconscious wish-fulfillment. You're afraid that I am going to see too clearly into the latency of your dreamwork."

I ignored him and went on relentlessly. "It came to me, then, that neither the man nor the woman could be the danger in the house, or they would not have locked and bolted themselves in their rooms. There must be, I realized, an unidentified menace. I decided to lock and bolt the door of my own room against this nameless threat, but, as you may have guessed, there was no lock, or key, or bolt. Furthermore, the door swung clear of the jamb by a good two inches. I looked about, a little wildly, and saw on a table what appeared to be the very mechanism the woman had held in her hand. I could not figure out all of its parts, but one of them was a blue pencil, a steely blue pencil,

64

and another seemed to be a bottle capper."

"The woman was, of course, a surrogate for your wife, or some other woman in a position of authority in your life, given to criticism of your work, and to her well-founded suspicion that you drink too much, far too much," Dr. Prell said.

"On another table," I went on coolly, "I saw a kit of tools, which I thought were carpenter's tools. I picked up three of these, and discovered that what I held was a cold chisel, an acetylene torch, and a drill. In other words—"

"A set of burglar's tools," said Dr. Prell.

I lit a cigarette and took a long inhale. "Precisely," I said. "I then took off my shoes and started to walk softly toward the woman's room. The sense of menace was gone. You see—"

"*You* were the danger in the house," said Dr. Prell.

"Were you going to kill this woman, or what?" It was my wife's voice, tinged with a familiar suspicion.

"You have been eavesdropping," I said.

"So have I," said Harriet Prell. "Alice and I were both listening. How did it come out?"

The ladies sat down on a davenport, each with a glass of brandy-and-Benedictine.

"I woke up," I said. "I always do in such a case. Even with tools, I can never get *at* the woman in my dreams."

"Goes back to childish fumblings, juvenile frustration, present insecurity," said Dr. Prell, pedantically, as if I were a couch patient. "To be sure, it is not always easy to separate the urge to ravish from the wish to destroy. They are, in fact, often conjoined, as we all know. In this case, we have the chisel and the drill on the one hand, the acetylene torch on the other. I am being deliberately overbasic," he added, patronizingly.

"I don't think the woman was me," Alice said. "I wouldn't bolt my door against you, darling, would I?"

"Some women bolt and run, others run and bolt," I said, and Dr. Prell made a gesture of irritation. "Obfuscatory," he murmured absently.

I poured myself some more brandy and said, "After you have gone, Alice will jump all over me for telling you about the woman in white, so I might as well explain another phenomenon of this particular dream. The lady had, then, two locks, one in the middle of her forehead and the other just above her heart. The first represented, of course, intellectual companionship, and the other a somewhat warmer consolation. I—"

"George invents things just to try to get me down," Alice said. "He never has the key to anything, and we're either locked out of the house at night or can't get the car started, or something."

"The key to a woman is not easy to find," said Dr. Prell,

a bit stuffily, I thought. He had walked, so to speak, right into a literary trap I had set for him.

"Ah, what a dusty answer gets the soul when hot for certain keys in this our life," I said.

"All I get at breakfast nowadays is Meredith," Alice said, with a small sigh.

"All I actually wanted to do," I said quickly, "was to tell the lady, 'Never shake thy gaudy locks at me.'" None of them, I could tell from their blank expressions, got this rather neat paraphrase, and that annoyed me.

"Speaking of dreams," Harriet began, "the other night I called on the President of the United States at the White House, but it wasn't Kennedy. It was an American Indian. His desk was piled high with papers, and he kept saying, 'How.'"

"Elementary," Dr. Prell began. "You see—"

"You are afraid the President has lost his sense of Know-how," I put in.

"My God, is he going to turn to Harriet for help?" Dr. Prell exclaimed. "If so, we are even more lost than I had feared."

"I haven't remembered any dreams for years," Alice said. "One of the last I remember was eight years ago, not long after we were married."

"Not the one about the blonde," I protested.

Alice gave a little shiver of disdain. "I can see her as plainly now as I did then," she said. "A horrible woman. You," she said to me, "were wearing a mask, and I don't blame you, for nobody would want to be recognized with such a frump." She turned to Dr. Prell. "It was in the lobby of a hotel," she told him. "I was sitting in a chair when the two of them came in and got on the elevator. My charming husband glanced at his wristwatch and said to me, 'We won't be a minute.' Then the elevator door closed and up they went."

"Alice has reproached me for eight years because of that incident," I said. "I have never worn a wristwatch, and I don't prefer blondes."

"After all, Alice, the dream was *yours*," Dr. Prell said. "It is true, of course, that the unconscious mind is extraordinarily perceptive, even intuitive, but it does make mistakes. It can be unfair as a result of jealousy, or some other common female frailty."

"I think she wanted to unmask my ideology at the time," I said. "I wouldn't tell her how I was going to vote that year."

"You can't get out of it that easily," my wife said. "What did you *do* upstairs?"

"My fair companion was an etcher and wanted to show me her etchings," I said, a little too casually. "They were the usual run-of-the-mill stuff, a few flowers, as I recall it, red roses and the like, and one or two rather bad jobs she had done on the châteaux of the Loire."

"I don't believe a word of it," Alice said. She had, I could tell, been drinking more brandy-and-Benedictine than was good for me. I thought we should all have highballs now, instead of more brandy, and I set about making them. "In the early 1950's, before McCarthage delenda was, I had some terrible nightmares," I said. "In them the menace in Washington and the menace in the home were all mixed up. Alice was always giving parties in my dreams, and I was always showing up with six, or sex, blondes, who were pure, or impure, creations of her suspicious mind. Her behavior at these parties was downright subversive. There were always such characters on hand as Benedict Arnold, Major André, Aaron Burr, and Simon Girty. She didn't know it, and I have never told her before, but the caterer's men were all government agents." I passed the highballs around. "Alice has a dossier in my dreams as long as your arm," I said.

"I wouldn't ask anybody to a party of mine named Simon Girty because I've never heard of anybody named Simon Girty," Alice said. "He's just making this all up. He's trying to make me forget about that awful woman at the elevator." She turned to Harriet. "You never saw such a get-up in your whole life," she said. "Everything was hiked up in front and pulled down behind."

"We had been wrassling in the taxi, not to put too fine a point on it," I confessed.

Dr. Prell had fairly gulped his drink, and so I made him another one. "For years," he said, "there has been a certain woman who recurs in my dreams. For reasons I shall not bother to detail, I had figured her as a surrogate for Harriet. Then, one night, Harriet walked in on us."

"Caught you cold, eh?" I asked.

"I don't like evenings like this," Harriet said. "Who was she, if she wasn't me?"

"You don't have to answer that question," I said hastily. "Shall I put 'The Sweetheart of Sigma Chi' on the Victrola? If the moonlight beams on the girl of your dreams, perhaps we can all figure out who she is."

"She was chewing gum," Alice said suddenly, and we all looked at her.

"The blonde at the elevator," I explained.

"Juicy Fruit," Alice added, and held out her empty glass. "He probably *still* sees her."

"If I couldn't meet a better class of women than Alice throws at me in her dreams, I would become a monk," I said with some finality.

"When did you first begin seeing that woman that you say you thought was me?" Harriet asked her husband. Dr. Prell tried to look owlish, but didn't quite bring it off. Comedy is scarcely his field.

"After all, I have been behaving properly in Alice's dreams for eight years now. Haven't I?" I demanded.

"Only because I can't remember my dreams, that's why," Alice said. "What does a long white dress mean in a dream, Morton?"

"Virginity," said Dr. Prell.

"Virginity, my foot," said Alice. "I think she was a female obstetrician. Disbarred," she added.

"Then what do you make of the acetylene torch?" Dr. Prell asked her.

"Fundamental," I said before she could answer. "Tigress, tigress burning bright in the forest of the nightie."

"I can't stand him when he gets cute," Alice said, putting me in the third person, always a sign of chill and trouble. "I don't know why the hell he doesn't teach palmistry. At night, maybe, on the third floor of an old school building somewhere."

"Without a fire escape?" I demanded.

"I couldn't care less whether it has or hasn't," she said, and I made a round of drinks that none of us needed.

"Men are always making things harder than they really are," Alice said. "They explain dreams exactly the same way they explain where they haven't been when any woman knows they have. You can't tell me that blonde hussy had anything whatever to do with infancy exhibitions. Any woman would know, any wife, that it could mainly be what is in George's mind when he's grown up."

"Now we go into clairvoyance and the subjunctive," I said, and Morton Prell and I exchanged knowing glances.

"What did you *do* with this woman that you always say you thought was me?" Harriet demanded.

"What did *you* do with Big Chief How How?" Dr. Prell demanded in his turn, his voice pitched a little high.

"I hate obscuringism," Alice said, obscurely.

"I know what you mean," said Harriet, who didn't.

"Dreams," said Dr. Prell, standing up, "should not be made the subject of too much levity. Come, Harriet, we must be going."

"Sit down a minute," I said. "It isn't late, and I want to tell you something I just remembered about one of those subversive parties Alice was always giving in my dreams."

"You didn't just remember it," Alice said. "You just made it up."

"In one of these party dreams—it was a party on our lawn—I had a hell of a time getting away from John Wilkes Booth," I said, "but I knew I had to get away, so that I could hide certain books here in this library."

Morton Prell perked up. "Interesting," he said. "What books?"

"Wait till I tell you," I said. "When I got in here, Long John Silver was standing right over there, holding a copy of *Traitor Island.*"

"Long John Silver is always in his nightmares," Alice put in, "because he read about him when he was eight years old."

"*Very* interesting," said Dr. Prell. "Silver's crutch is, of course, a symbol of your need for help."

"Nonsense," I said. "It is a symbol of *his* need for help."

"Quibble quabble," said Harriet. "If something isn't hard, men will make it hard. Everything dual is always oneness in idioms," she added fuzzily. "She has a sharp eye, she has a keen ear, and she has a light hand with a cake and a nose for news."

"That would have to be a nostril for news," her husband said.

"I took the book away from Silver," I said, returning to my story, "and hid it behind a stack of others. Then I noticed, to my horror, that the titles of a lot of other familiar books had changed. I saw *Un-American Tragedy* by Dreiser, *Alias in Wonderland,* and *Look Homeward, Agent,* for instance."

"He's worked on that one for days. I can tell," Alice said.

"It does seem contrived," said Dr. Prell, "but the unconscious mind is most inventive, most inventive."

"I want to get back to my library dream," I cut in impatiently. "I heard the caterer's men coming, and I hastily hid a book with the title *Lincoln's Doctor's Dossier.* I took it out from the books beginning with L and stuck it under another letter. You can guess what one, can't you, Morton?" I asked.

"Oh?" said Morton.

"Not at all," I said. "Lincoln, as we know, became, in our age of political suspicion, unfairly associated with subversive organizations. As the caterer's men came into the library, I whispered to Silver, 'Now he belongs to the H's.'"

"Remarkable," said Dr. Prell. He stood up again and said, "Now we *must* go, Harriet."

"Not until I explain to you illiterates why Long John Silver gets into my nightmares," I said. "His deadliest enemy in *Treasure Island* happens to be a man named George Merry. Near the end of the book Silver shoots George Merry and kills him. That scared me when I was eight years old and it still scares me, apparently."

"Unfamiliarity with children's books does not constitute

illiteracy," Morton Prell said stiffly as he reached the door.

After we had said goodnight, Alice fled upstairs without a word. I went back to the library and finished my drink slowly. Then I went up and tried the door of Alice's bedroom. It was neither locked nor bolted.

"*You* are the danger in the house," I told her. "I just wanted to explain the long white dress. You always wear a long white nightgown. In short, white is the color of my true love's dress."

"Shut up," she said. When Alice says shut up at that hour of the night, she means it. I shut up.

10

Look Out for the Thing

ᔕᔕᔕᔕᔕᔕᔕᔕᔕᔕᔕᔕᔕᔕᔕᔕᔕᔕᔕᔕᔕᔕᔕᔕᔕᔕᔕᔕᔕᔕᔕᔕ

A crooked mile from my house, and up a woodland road, there is a sign that reads "Look Out for the Thing." I don't know who put up the sign—a mischievous child, perhaps, or a waggish adult, or maybe the estranged wife of the Thing. Passers-by, on foot or in Ford, laugh at the warning, but not as merrily as they used to. The autumn picnicker, homing in the early dusk, may pale a little at sudden sight of the black beware, pointing its bony finger at oblivious October asleep in its red and yellow coverlet, dreaming of old and more tranquil Octobers, famous for their drinking songs, their jolly jack-o'-lanterns, and their lyric moons. But he will shrug it off, and walk on whistling in the gathering gloom, confident in his silly superstition that there is not a Thing in the darkening woods. My French poodle and I know, of course, that the picnicker is living in a picnicker's paradise. The poodle has seen the Thing and so have I, too many times.

The first time, for the poodle, was when she was only nine months old. We were walking along a country road when she suddenly saw the Thing, walking toward us, a hundred yards away. My four-footed French friend trembled, snorted like a cornered fawn, and abruptly tore off across a meadow and into the woods. What she had seen, at long and dim distance, for a dog, was an eight-year-old boy. He had become magnified in capricious vision to enormous size. Such an apparition, cloudily seen and wildly imagined, was too much for the poodle, and she sought in the woods the comforting company of less ominous and menacing creatures.

Yes, Virginia, there is a Thing, older than the Questing Beast, uglier than the Loch Ness monster. It speaks in many tongues and sleeps in many minds. It invades the world and mind of Man, inhabits headlines, feeds on limelight, and attacks its prey in the dark. It can't tell black from white, since it sees only red, and it tires quickly when digging for facts because they often lie deep at the roots of truth, and the Thing has learned to nourish itself on suspicions, guesses, and old accusations, that it finds wherever it looks. It likes to trumpet defiance from a high peak of immunity, but when its prey challenges it to stand forth and fight, it quietly disappears.

The Thing has great power and vast ingenuity, for it can

make guilt out of many things, out of whatever comes to hand, in fact: association, accusation, appearance, aspect, attitude, and even ability; dedication, devotion, duty, and even a man's courageous determination to speak his mind in the interest of the welfare of his country. The Thing can blacken a man at a distance of ten thousand miles, by using one or another of its many stings: the thundering charge, the sweeping generalization, the bold assumption, the mysterious record, the secret testimony, the overheard insinuation, the patriotic gesture, the enormous lie, the fearful warning. The Thing can jump a mile to conclusions, crying, as it passes the microphones, "Look, Mom, I'm denouncing!"

The Thing's worst effect is upon the rational mind of Man. It enlarges his credulity by magnifying peril, exaggerating fear, and inventing danger. Busy as a bowerbird, it will build for man, free of charge, a new wing for his skepticism, a left wing, or a right wing, so poorly lighted and so full of shadows that Man cannot tell mouse from monster, friend from foe, or truth from tommyrot, and is likely to fire wildly in the dark when the Thing cries, "There he goes!" One of the Thing's most brilliant achievements, however, was to make Man lose his faith in the practice and precept of innocence by exoneration. Now a man may be considered guilty even after he has been proven innocent. Now the scarlet letter A may stand for the awful word "Acquitted," and now Man, in his abject confusion, is likely to point out exonerated patriots on the street and whisper, "There goes the accused." The Thing can make Man do even worse than that. It can persuade him to protect free speech by keeping it securely bottled up, so that it cannot be dangerously used by such dubious citizens as the Accused, the Exonerated, and the Acquitted.

The Thing teaches that the Defendant cannot be trusted, for he has been indelibly stained by subpoena, process, and probe. It suggests that anything he may say, or write, in his own defense is questionable and should be used against him.

A friend of mine contends that there should be state institutions in America for the incurably unfair, the violently prejudiced, and the criminally thoughtless, but I explained to him that this would deprive such persons of their right of free speech.

Upon this we had a silent and sombre drink together, and parted, saying to each other, "Look Out for the Thing." Do not attempt to take the Thing single-handed. It is armed and dangerous, and what is worse, it has a lot of friends.

11

The Future, If Any, of Comedy or, Where Do We Non-Go from Here?

I called the other afternoon on my old friend Graves Moreland, the Anglo-American literary critic—his mother was born in Ohio—who lives alone in a fairy-tale cottage on the Upson Downs, raising hell and peacocks, the former only when the venerable gentleman becomes an angry old man about the state of literature or something else that is dwindling and diminishing, such as human stature, hope, and humor.

My unscientific friend does not believe that human stature is measurable in terms of speed, momentum, weightlessness, or distance from earth, but is a matter of the development of the human mind. After Gagarin became the Greatest Man in the World, for a nation that does not believe in the cult of personality or in careerism, Moreland wrote me a letter in which he said: "I am not interested in how long a bee can live in a vacuum, or how far it can fly. A bee's place is in the hive."

"I have come to talk with you about the future of humor

and comedy," I told him, at which he started slightly, and then made us each a stiff drink, with a trembling hand.

"I seem to remember," he said, "that in an interview ten years ago you gave humor and comedy five years to live. Did you go to their funeral?"

"I was wrong," I admitted. "Comedy didn't die, it just went crazy. It has identified itself with the very tension and terror it once did so much to alleviate. We now have not only what has been called over here the comedy of menace but we also have horror jokes, magazines known as Horror Comics, and sick comedians. There are even publications called *Sick* and *Mad*. The *Zeitgeist* is not crazy as a loon or mad as a March hare; it is manic as a man."

"I woke up this morning," Moreland said, "paraphrasing Lewis Carroll. Do you want to hear the paraphrase?"

"Can I bear it?" I asked, taking a final gulp of my drink, and handing him the empty glass.

"Just barely," he said, and he repeated his paraphrase:

> "The time has come," the walrus said,
>   "To speak of manic things,
> Of shots and shouts, and sealing dooms
>   Of commoners and kings."

Moreland fixed us each another drink, and said, "For God's sake, tell me something truly amusing."

"I'll try," I said, and sat for a moment thinking. "Oh yes, the other day I reread some of Emerson's *English Traits,* and there was an anecdote about a group of English and Americans visiting Germany, more than a hundred years ago. In the railway station at Berlin, a uniformed attendant was chanting, 'Foreigners this way! Foreigners this way!' One woman—she could have been either English or American—went up to him and said, 'But *you* are the foreigners.'" I took a deep breath, and said, "I admit that going back to Ralph Waldo Emerson for humor is like going to a modern musical comedy for music and comedy."

"What's the matter with the music?" Moreland asked.

"It doesn't drown out the dialogue," I explained.

"Let's talk about books," Moreland said. "I am told that in America you have non-books by non-writers, brought out by non-publishers for non-readers. Is it all non-fiction?"

"There is non-fiction and non-non-fiction," I said. "Speaking of nonism: the other day, in a story about a sit-down demonstration, the Paris *Herald Tribune* wrote, 'The non-violence became noisier.' And then Eichmann was quoted as saying, in non-English, that Hitler's plan to exterminate the Jews was nonsense."

"If we cannot tell evil, horror, and insanity from nonsense, what is the future of humor and comedy?" Moreland asked, grimly.

"Cryptic," I said. "They require, for existence, a brave spirit and a high heart, and where do you find these? In our present era of Science and *Angst*, the heart has been downgraded, to use one of our popular retrogressive verbs."

"I know what you mean," Moreland sighed. "Last year your Tennessee Williams told our Dilys Powell, in a television program, that it is the task of the playwright to throw light into the dark corners of the human heart. Like almost everybody else, he confused the heart, both as organ and as symbol, with the disturbed psyche, the deranged glands, and the jumpy central nervous system. I'm not pleading for the heart that leaps up when it beholds a rainbow in the sky, or for the heart that with rapture fills and dances with the daffodils. The sentimental pure heart of Galahad is gone with the knightly years, but I still believe in the heart of the George Meredith character that was not made of the stuff that breaks."

"We no longer have Tom Moore's and Longfellow's 'heart for any fate,' either," I said.

"Moore and Longfellow didn't have the fate that faces us," Moreland said. "One day our species promises coexistence, and the next day it threatens coextinction." We sat for a while drinking in silence.

"The heart," I said finally, "is now either in the throat or the mouth or the stomach or the shoes. When it was worn in the breast, or even on the sleeve, we at least knew where it was." There was another long silence.

"You have visited England five times in the past quarter-century, I believe," my host said. "What has impressed you most on your present visit?"

"I would say depressed, not impressed," I told him. "I should say it is the turning of courts of law into veritable theatres for sex dramas, involving clergymen and parishioners, psychiatrists and patients. It is becoming harder and harder to tell law courts and political arenas from the modern theatre."

"Do you think we need a new Henry James to re-explore the Anglo-American scene?" he asked. "Or perhaps a new Noël Coward?"

"But you must have heard it said that the drawing room disappeared forever with the somnolent years of James and the antic heyday of Coward. I myself hear it said constantly —in drawing rooms. In them, there is usually a group of Anglo-Americans with tragicomic problems, worthy of being explored either in the novel or in the play or in comedy and satire." I stood up and began pacing.

"If you are trying to get us out of the brothel, the dustbin, the kitchen sink, and the tawdry living room, you are probably wasting your time," Moreland told me. "Too many of our writers seem to be interested only in creatures that crawl out of the woodwork or from under the rock."

"Furiouser and furiouser," I said. "I am worried about the current meanings of the word 'funny.' It now means ominous, as when one speaks of a funny sound in the motor; disturbing, as when one says that a friend is acting funny; and frightening, as when a wife tells the police that it is funny, but her husband hasn't been home for two days and nights."

Moreland sat brooding for a full minute, during which I made each of us a new drink. He took his glass, clinked it against mine, and said, "*Toujours gai*, what the hell!" borrowing a line from Don Marquis' Mehitabel.

"Be careful of the word 'gay,' for it, too, has undergone a change. It now means, in my country, homosexual," I said. "Oh, I forgot to say that if one is taken to the funny house in the funny wagon, he is removed to a mental institution in an ambulance. Recently, by the way, I received a questionnaire in which I was asked whether or not I was non-institutionalized."

My host went over and stared out the window at his peacocks; then he turned to me. "Is it true that you believe the other animals are saner than the human species?"

"Oh, that is demonstrable," I told him. "Do you remember the woman in the French Alps who was all alone with her sheep one day when the sun darkened ominously? She told the sheep, 'The world is coming to an end!' And the sheep said—all in unison, I have no doubt—'Ba-a-a!' The sound mockery of sheep is like the salubrious horse laugh."

"That is only partly non-nonsense," he began.

"If you saw the drama called *Rhinoceros*," I said, "think of the effect it would have on an audience of rhinos when the actor on stage suddenly begins turning into a rhinoceros. The rhinos would panic, screaming 'Help!'—if that can be screamed in their language."

"You think the Russians are getting ahead of us in comedy?" Moreland demanded.

"Non-God, no!" I said. "The political and intellectual Left began fighting humor and comedy years ago, because they fear things they do not understand and cannot manage, such as satire and irony, such as humor and comedy. Nevertheless, like any other human being upon whom the spotlight of the world plays continually, Khrushchev, the anti-personality cultist, has become a comic actor, or thinks he has. In his famous meeting with Nixon a few years ago he seemed to believe that he was as funny as Ed Wynn. But, like Caesar, he has only one joke, so far as I can find out. It consists in saying, 'That would be sending the goat to look after the cabbage.' Why in the name of his non-God doesn't he vary it a bit?"

"Such as?" Moreland asked.

"Such as 'sending the cat to guard the mice,' or 'the falcon to protect the dove,' or most terribly sharp of all, 'the human being to save humanity.'"

"You and I have fallen out of literature into politics," Moreland observed.

"What a nasty fall was there!" I said.

Moreland went over to stare at his peacocks again, and then came back and sat down, restively. "In our age of Science and *Angst*," he said, "it seems to me more brave to stay on Earth and explore inner man than to fly far from the sphere of our sorrow and explore outer space."

"The human ego being what it is," I put in, "science fiction has always assumed that the creatures on the planets of a thousand larger solar systems than ours must look like gigantic tube-nosed fruit bats. It seems to me that the first human being to reach one of these planets may well learn what it is to be a truly great and noble species."

84

"Now we are leaving humor and comedy behind again," Moreland protested.

"Not in the largest sense of the words," I said. "The other day Arnold Toynbee spoke against the inveterate tendency of our species to believe in the uniqueness of its religions, its ideologies, and its virtually everything else. Why do we not realize that no ideology believes so much in itself as it disbelieves in something else? Forty years ago an English writer, W. L. George, dealt with this subject in *Eddies of the Day*, and said, as an example, that 'Saint George for Merry England' would not start a spirit half so quickly as 'Strike frog-eating Frenchmen dead!' "

"There was also *Gott strafe Angleterre*," Moreland reminded me, "and *Carthago delenda est*, or if you will, *Deus strafe Carthage*. It isn't what the ideologist believes in, but what he hates, that puts the world in jeopardy. This is the force, in our time and in every other time, that urges the paranoiac and the manic-depressive to become head of a state. Complete power not only corrupts but it also attracts the mad. There is a bitter satire for a future writer in that."

"Great satire has always been clearly written and readily understandable," I said. "But we now find writers obsessed by the nooks and crannies of their ivory towers, and curiously devoted to the growing obscurity and complexity of poetry and non-poetry. I wrote a few years ago that one of the cardinal rules of writing is that the reader should be able to get some idea of what the story is about. If a poem, for example, is understandable only to its author, then Max Eastman's phrase, 'poets talking to themselves,' is not only accurate but alarming in a time like ours."

Moreland didn't say anything at first, but he made us another and stiffer drink.

"The Communists," he said, "may yet turn literature into a phase of modern technology. Some members of the Russian Society of Authors will simply have to push a button, and out will come a novel or a play. Incapable of revision—that is, change, growth, and development—and subject only to mechanistic favorable criticism, obtained by pushing another button in another machine. There is a satire in that for a future writer, if there is going to be a future."

"Modern psychology and psychiatry have made us all afraid of ourselves," I said abruptly. "*Angst* is spreading, and with it mental ailments of whose cause and cure, one authority has recently said, we know little or nothing. But the terminology of psychiatry proliferates to the point that almost everybody now seems to think he is schizophrenic, schizoid, or schizo. I expect any day to see the slang word 'skizzy' come into common use. A psychologist in America not long ago warned his colleagues at a convention that they were not so much arriving at cures as inventing new terms for the incurable. When neuro-psychotic became psychoneurotic, the verbiage was off to a flying start, startling too many people. I heard of one frightened woman who burst into her doctor's office crying, 'I think I have got psychotherapy!' The doctor was able to prove to her quite simply that she did not have that."

"Are you moving toward some basic conclusion?" Moreland asked.

"I was coming to another subject for present or future satire," I said. "That is the subject of the Area Man. We are divided into literally hundreds of Area Men, none of whom knows or cares very much about men in other categories of endeavor or thought. But we mumble along in our multiple confusion. Every man is now an island unto himself, interested in, even obsessed by, his own preoccupation. For example, I was agitated some twenty years ago when I discovered the gulf of ignorance that existed between the ophthalmologist and the psychologist. Each of them is concerned only with his own end of the optic nerve, which happens to join the eyeball and the brain. I have found out that the eye doctors and the mind doctors have developed a great many jokes and anecdotes about one another, without getting together and threshing things out. A certain male adult began seeing double, and he went to a psychiatrist, who decided that the man's problem lay in his inability to make up his mind as to which one of two girls he was in love with. The distracted fellow then called on a great eye man who cleared up the condition with certain eye drops. I told this story to our American humorist S. J. Perelman, and he said to me, 'The story is incomplete. Which girl *was* he in love with?' "

"I know of two classes of Area Men that certain authorities are trying to interfuse, as the science fiction writers say," Moreland told me. "Lord Hailsham was recently quoted as saying that all good scientists are poets, and Alfred North Whitehead made a strenuous attempt to find the scientist in Tennyson, Wordsworth, and Shelley. He even wrote, 'If Shelley had been born a hundred years later, there would have been a Newton among chemists.' "

"Shelley in the bells and grass, Shelley with an apple halfway to his head," I murmured, but my host went me a couple better.

"My heart leaps up when I behold a test tube in the lab!" he cried. "And did you once see Shelley plain? And was he stained with chemicals?"

"If Shelley was a scientist, then I am a neuro-surgeon," I said. "Any scientist knows that the moth cannot desire the star, for the simple scientific reason that the moth cannot see the star. What the moth desires is the street lamp, the candle flame, the light in the window. Too bad Whitehead did not rewrite the great lyric for the sake of modern science."

"I weep for the man that wept for Adonais," Moreland sighed.

We both walked over to the window and stared out at the peacocks again.

"Don't ask me how we are going to get out of the present dehumanization of our species," I told him, "because I don't know. I am glad to say, to quote Poe, that it is neither beast nor human, it is neither man nor woman, that wakes me every morning at my quiet hotel in London. It is a blackbird, who begins to sing as the clock strikes five. You see—"

But Moreland wanted to show me that he could quote from the poets, too, and he did so:

> The nightingale has a lyre of gold,
> The lark's is a clarion call,
> And the blackbird plays but a boxwood flute,
> But I love him best of all.

We went back and sat down.

"There is, thank God," I said, "no such thing as a de-blackbirdization."

"Would you like to see a world conference of Area Men?" Moreland asked. "If so, do not expect me to attend. There is enough Babel and Bedlam the way it is, and an organization called the United Notions would get us nowhere even faster than we are now going, which is seventeen hundred miles a minute, I believe. Such a convention might even lead to the First Word War."

"Well, at any rate," I said, "you have suggested good titles for a satire, *The United Notions* and *The First Word War*. There are plenty of ideas lying around, but what we lack is wordmen, as they are called in Hollywood, to write about them."

"Let's get back to *Angst* for a moment," my host said.

"On the contrary, let's get away from *Angst* for good," I objected. "In a review of what he called unscientific science fiction, Kingsley Amis spoke of 'the threadbare convention of telepathy.' Now, I have studied and practiced mental telepathy for sixty years, and its existence is demonstrable. The present *Angst,* the *Zeitgeist* of the moment, is quite simply, it seems to me, the product of mass mental projection of gloom. I have traced its depressing effects during the past two years. In that period I have got a dismaying increase of letters from friends and strangers of all ages, telling of the onset of *Angst*. They use such expressions as anxiety, nameless dread, and even *heulendes Elend,* which is German for the sobbing miseries. Too many people have now got everything from the galloping jumps to the mumbling crumbles, and they are contagious. I have no doubt that telepathy has become a threadbare convention of science fiction, but it is, alas, a monstrous human fact."

"Let's go and look at the peacocks again," Moreland sighed, and we both went over to the window.

"I have a theory of my own about the spread of *Angst,*" Moreland said finally. "We talk too much about this damnable dehumanization, and the process shows up in too many of the dramas and novels of our day. Love has become a four-letter word, and sex is no longer creative but destructive. We are assured, by some authorities, that the normal is a matter of mass behavior, but the normal can never be synonymous with the average, the majority, the customary,

89

or the habitual. The normal is that which functions in accordance with its design, and in sex, and its inversions and perversions, however popular, we seem to overlook the design of the morphology and biology of the human being."

"You are oversimplifying," I told him, "but it is refreshing in an age of overcomplication."

"A long time ago we began calling this century the Age of Anxiety and the Aspirin Age," Moreland went on. "Your late President Roosevelt, thirty years ago, said that the only thing to fear is fear itself, thus giving the psychiatrist a new term, phobophobia. President Eisenhower spoke so often about the danger of fear and hysteria that he planted them in the consciousness of his television listeners. And then *Time* Magazine not long ago devoted its cover story to an article called 'The Anatomy of *Angst*.' How can we mentally jam all this broadcasting of gloom?"

"By rising above it," I said. "By the lifting of the spirit, by what Dorothy Thompson called, in her last book, 'The Courage to Be Happy.' It takes guts to be happy, make no mistake about it; and I don't mean slap-happy, or drink-happy, or drug-happy."

"We are told that the balance of power in the world, and its maintenance, are realistic, but the realistic is not always the true," Moreland said. "The greatest truth of our time is both simple and awful—total war means annihilation, and the Brink of War has become the Brink of Was."

"I wish I had said that," I murmured. "Power, incidentally, also tends to make men stupid. When Mikoyan visited the United States, he asked more than one worker, 'Do you want war?' They all said no, but bitter irony would have been the proper weapon, if irony were not so dangerous in this age of non-communication. The answer to Mikoyan should have been, 'Yes, of course. I should like to be killed,

90

and have my wife and children killed, and all my friends
and neighbors, and my city destroyed.' "

"We have come a long way from humor and comedy this
afternoon," Moreland sighed.

"On the contrary," I said, "we are just getting around
to it. Without satire no civilization can be truly described
or benefited. We could name many names, from Voltaire to
Swift, before we ran into the modern morbid playwrights
and sex novelists, who are more interested in the sordid
corners of life than in the human heart."

"You mean the non-heart," Moreland said. "Have you
counted the recent books that deal with the human condi-

tion, or predicament, or tragedy?"

"Yes," I said, "and I even remember when we wrote about the bright human spectacle, and the human comedy. If there is no human comedy it will be necessary to create one. How long can the needle of the human gramophone stay in the rut of *Angst* without wearing out and ending in the repetition of a ghoulish gibbering?"

I glanced at my wristwatch and saw that it was time to go. Moreland took me to the door, and we shook hands. I had a final thought, and said to my host: "I think we must learn to brighten the human idiom, as well as to make it communicable."

"I'll let you have the last word," he sighed.

"All right, then," I said. "Life at the moment is a tale told in an idiom, full of unsoundness and fury, signifying nonism. The other day I read a love scene in a story that went like this: 'Am I beautiful?' she asked him. 'Terribly,' he said. And then he asked her, 'Do you love me?' 'Horribly,' she said."

"Why don't you go home and write something humorous?" Graves Moreland demanded. "Don't you want to?"

"Frightfully," I told him, and I wandered slowly o'er the lea, wondering if the modern world had lost a great nuclear physicist when Thomas Gray died in the wrong century.

12

Foreword to Fifth New Yorker Album

In prefaces to previous collections of *New Yorker* drawings practically everything that could possibly interest anyone about how the artists work, where the ideas come from, etc., has been gone into. It leaves this Foreword to the Fifth Album, therefore—unless somebody has a question— little more than a ritual, like the cry of "Linesmen ready?" before the start of a tennis match. ·

If there were a question, I suppose it would be: what do people really want, anyway? As a matter of fact, that question is often asked of the editors. It invariably leaves them nonplussed. They do not, the secret is, exactly know what they want. I have in mind one of them who went to F.A.O. Schwarz to buy a toy for his infant daughter, who didn't know what she wanted, either, but who wanted something. A saleslady handed him, rather abruptly, a little woolly lamb with a bell around its neck. "Would a soft animal help you?" she asked. This simple question had a curious effect. The editor began to feel sorry for himself. His own vague yearnings, instead of his child's, became uppermost in his mind. In the end he bought a soft animal, but he never took it home; he set it up on his desk at the office. He doesn't know whether it has helped him or not.

It is much the same with the drawings that are submitted. The personal idiosyncrasies of the picture selectors become mixed up with the ill-defined requirements of the magazine and with the figured predilections of its readers. (Sometimes these last are figured one way and sometimes another, depending on nobody knows exactly what.) The result is an amorphous and hazy state of mind out of which it is difficult to fetch up a coherent and succinct answer to the question "What do you want?"

Nor will it do much good to turn to the drawings themselves for some idea of what is wanted. No definition of suitability, based on the pictures herein contained, would be safe to go by. Suitability is here one year and gone the next. Take the drawing of the dirigible that inadvertently sailed for Athens, Greece, instead of Athens, Georgia, and also the drawing of the powerboat that was delivered to a gentleman's Adirondack estate by mistake. It might be adduced from these that what is wanted is pictures wherein people are seen going thousands of miles out of their way with cumbersome objects. And yet a picture of an absent-minded attaché of the Smithsonian Institution showing up for work in the State of Washington, rather than the District of Columbia, would most certainly be rejected, even though he were presented as having made the trip with a stuffed whale. This is partly owing to the law of diminishing desire, and partly owing to a lot of nuances.

A few general suggestions might be offered, however, based on certain immutable differences between men and women, as the editors see them. Women, it will be discovered, may be treated any which way so long as they are not permitted to descend to the profounder depths of iso-

lation and futility. These depths are reserved for male characters. An illustration in point is the picture of the little man wandering around among the gay and oblivious guests at a large party and beseeching somebody to "Pick a card, any card." Here the peculiar capacity of the male for achieving an almost sublime loneliness has been poignantly portrayed. He has got himself into a situation which the female, with her inexorable demands upon awareness, could not conceivably get into. If a woman asks somebody to pick a card, somebody is going to pick a card.

A sort of map for artists might be drawn, showing that women live in Arcady—sometimes, to be sure, a fool's

Arcady, but Arcady nevertheless—a place of trim lawns and straight streets. Touching this Arcady, as the Bois de Boulogne touches Paris, is Jeopardy, the haunt of the male. In its dark woods he becomes inextricably entangled: he rows his boat in a crew race up the wrong branch of the river; he drives his golf ball into the inviolate gardens of imperious ladies; he dresses up in masquerade costume and goes to the wrong hotel; he calls his home on the phone and the dog answers.

What, it may be asked, of the offspring of these people, what of the children who are to become the men and women of tomorrow's *New Yorker* albums? I find, in examining the drawings, that it is safe to represent them as having the upper hand, or just about to get the upper hand, as in the picture where the father calls his son's "bluff" in the poker hand. No father, viewing that picture, will have any doubt but that the little fellow has a full house as against papa's three of a kind. Various individuals

96

and societies have requested *The New Yorker* to strike a note of hope in the domestic scene, pointing out that modern methods of child education have restored control to the parents. This *The New Yorker* has not found to be true. When and if the time comes that fathers can be counted on to win the best two upper hands out of three, *The New Yorker* will be the first to recognize the trend.

Several other conclusions as to what is wanted might be drawn, or jumped at, from the pictures in this collection, but I do not see that they would serve any special purpose at this time. For one thing, the Upswing is at hand, and it is probably going to change human nature a great deal; if it doesn't, the Collapse of Civilization, which is just around the corner, will.

In conclusion, the editors wish gratefully to thank the artists for all they have been through in helping to create this sensitive and far-reaching record of adventure and misadventure in a great city, a crazy world, and an incomprehensible life.

13

Carpe Noctem, If You Can

ᎧᎧᎧᎧᎧᎧᎧᎧᎧᎧᎧᎧᎧᎧᎧᎧᎧᎧᎧᎧᎧᎧᎧᎧᎧᎧᎧᎧᎧᎧᎧᎧᎧᎧᎧᎧᎧᎧᎧ

About once a month, after dinner, I gird up my loins, such as they are, take as deep a breath as I can, throw my shoulders back as far as they will go now, walk into the room with the television set, boldly turn it on, picking a channel at random, and then see how long I can stand it. One night I could stand it for less than a minute. A choco-late-flavored narrator began by saying, "The strongest human emotion is a mother's desire for a baby of her own." Well, to begin with, if she is a mother, she *has* a baby of her own, and my old ears are still sharp enough to be afflicted by the crumbling of precision and sense. But this minor flaw was not what caused me to turn off the set.

I do not question the literal truth of the narrator's state-ment, in view of the alarming and easily available vital statistics that support it: every twenty-four hours 288,000 babies are born on our planet, and there will be some five million blessed events in the United States alone this year. What really got me was the narrator's next sentence, and the action that immediately followed it. He said, "This story, strangely enough, begins in violence." Now what in

98

the name of heaven is strange about violence today in any area whatever, on or off television? No sooner had the narrator made his strange statement than all hell broke loose on the screen. A group of people suddenly began beating the holy bejudas out of each other, and there was the sound of body blows, grunts, and heavy breathing with which so many cop-and-murder television shows begin. I quickly silenced the box and put an old Bing Crosby record on the Victrola.

The dangers inherent in discussing dramas of mother love that begin with scenes of violence must be apparent to anyone who is aware of the real, or fancied, craving of television audiences for blood and brutality. Perhaps I should not go so far as to outline some of these dangers, but if I don't, somebody else is bound to. Among the popular stories of the American past that might be revived in violence for television programs are those involving the Little Colonel, Molly Makebelieve, Peg o' my Heart, Rebecca of Sunnybrook Farm, Pollyanna, the Little Minister, Little Lord Fauntleroy, the Choir Invisible, Beside the Bonnie Brier Bush, the Little Shepherd of Kingdom Come, the Rover Boys, the Bobbsey Twins, and Nize Baby. I am afraid that the televisionaries may decide that millions of televiewers would simply love to watch a program begin with a scene in which a sainted mother or child bride kicks Lord Fauntleroy in the stomach.

To an ancient rememberer like me, the field of old-fashioned books and characters that could be beaten to death on television is a vast one, and includes, I am certain, hundreds that no television executive ever read or heard about: the novels of F. Marion Crawford, *V. V.'s Eyes*, *Freckles*, *The House of a Thousand Candles*, *The Inside of the Cup*, *Black Beauty*, Penrod, Sam, Willie Baxter, *The*

Harvester, Helen's Babies, Editha's Burglar, The Five Little Peppers, and on and on. (Now, lookit, Television, while I shake my gory locks at you. We could work into them old books a sadistic police lieutenant, see? They ain't no limit to the mayhem and mangling we could get into 'em. All that them books need to make 'em fit for modern consumption is cops and murder, and crazy guys on the prowl at night, get it?)

Well, let them go ahead with the debauchery of some of these old stories, and we shall see what will happen. I would not have brought the matter up if I did not see a ray of hope. Now that practically everybody is rioting around the world, what is to prevent the fifteen million American men and women now sixty-five years old or older from rising up in angry unison and beating the holy bejudas out of television? It is, as comforting thoughts go nowadays, a comforting thought. Millions of sentimental oldsters, devoted admirers of *Prunella, The Wizard of Oz,* Owen Meredith's *Lucile, Snow White,* David Grayson's *Adventures in Contentment, A Girl of the Limberlost, The Winning of Barbara Worth,* and the books of Ralph Henry Barbour, would surely riot in a body and descend on the networks if their old favorites were turned into bloody shambles. (I neither suggest, nor approve of, the use of guns or knives, brickbats or ball bats, but it does seem to me that an old-fashioned egg fight, with both sides armed only with that weapon, might settle something, might undehumanize television's bloody bang-bangs, or, at the very least, give the management of television channels pause. If we cannot obtain surcease, we could at least find some comfort in pause.)

It is worth thinking about, if you don't think about it at night when you are trying to sleep. I was trying to sleep the other night when I suddenly began thinking about it again. I realized, lying there, that television men might be stimulated by this essay to brutalize *Peter Pan, Peter Rabbit, The Wind in the Willows, The Crock of Gold,* and also to do violence to some of the inviolable old Alices of literature. I thought, I regret to say, and probably should not report, of *Alice Threw the Looking Glass* and *Alice-Spit-in-the-Fire,* and then got up and had a stiff drink and a cigarette after this paraphrase leaped into my naughty mind: "O won't you dismember Sweet Alice, Ben Bolt?"

I got back in bed, and pulled the sheet over my head, but the unguided missiles of midnight meditation got me up again. I had begun rewriting the opening sentences of a couple of books and of one beloved poem. Evelyn Waugh's "They were still dancing" became "They were still punching," and the first line of Sabatini's *Scaramouche* —"He was born with the gift of laughter and a sense that the world is mad"—twisted itself into "He was born with the gift of slaughter and a sense that the word is Sade." But what really brought me incurably wide awake and out of bed for the rest of the untender night was " 'Twas the fight before Christmas, when all through the house, Every creature was sparring, including a mouse."

My trouble, as you can see, is the gift of total recall. Thought association, for the total recaller, is endless and often cruel, particularly in the mind of an ancient who is a victim of chronic word garbling. Such a mind, prowling at night, can turn *A Window in Thrums* into *A Widow in Slums,* and *When Knighthood Was in Flower* into *When Girlhood Was Deflowered.* What is worse, the nocturnal mind that fossicks (look it up in the OED) may get around to *Little Boy Blew His Top* and *The Pie-eyed Peeper of Hamlin.*

Now, please do not write me and tell me the name of
your psychiatrist. I do not have a psychiatrist and I do not
want one, for the simple reason that if he listened to me
long enough, he might become disturbed. I say this with
unreassuring confidence because of the effect an outline of
the present essay had upon a psychologist friend of mine
who came to a dinner party at my house when my thoughts
on the subject were in the formative phase.

When I had finished talking, the psychologist, whom I
shall call Dr. Winterhorn, sat in a corner for a while,
brooding over his fifth Scotch highball. Then he called to
me, and I went over and sat beside him. Since he is also
in his sixties and has considerable, if not total recall, he

had been silently conjuring up names in old books and stories that I had left out. "You do not mention the televised violence that might be done to other old fictional characters," he began. "You leave out Frank Merriwell, Tom Swift, Buster Brown, and the Brushwood Boy, to name only four." Thereupon, being a psychologist, he began lecturing. "I think that your own clinging to the somnolent and sentimental past is perhaps an indication that you do not realize that the nature of violence, like the nature of humor and comedy, has changed with each decade of this turbulent century, and, on television, is not so much a deliberate or intentional device of writers, producers, and network owners as it is an unconscious projection of the effect upon all of us, or most of us, of the *Zeitgeist,* or protean spirit of the changing age." His voice was rising now and he stood up as if at a lectern. But I can lecture too, and I was a couple of highballs ahead of him.

"You named in your list only male fictional characters of the past," I said, getting a note of suspicion in my voice. "Why do you leave out Daisy, of the bicycle built for two, Little Annie Rooney, and Sweet Rosie O'Grady? All these long-lost girls were what my mother used to call as pure as the driven snow, and the mugging and manhandling of them could be brought to a high point of terror on television—or should I just say terrorvision?"

"Those silly and ridiculous old American sentimental songs give me the creeps," said Dr. Winterhorn. "When I was a little boy my father made me nervous by singing 'And that's a pretty good sign that she's your Tootsie Wootsie in the good old summertime,' and—"

"There is also a Tootsie Wootsie," I reminded him, "in 'Meet Me in St. Louis, Louie,' but it is somewhat offset by

103

a mild rhythmic violence of the period known as the hootchy-kootchy."

He seemed nettled, in the manner of all interrupted lecturers. "Let us not go back," he said severely, "to the turkey trot, the grizzly bear, and the honey bug."

"Freudian slip!" I exclaimed. "You meant to say the bunny hug." I extended my arms toward him and said, "Shall we ball the jack?" This clearly upset him and he sat down abruptly. The hour was late now. The teetotallers and light drinkers had departed, but the rest of us had reached the point of no retire and were in for Long Night's Journey into Day. Dr. Winterhorn and I were both brought another highball.

"Let us strive to thresh this matter out," said the doctor, who always forgets that he is a man of habit patterns, and that he and I, after night has fallen, but dawn has not yet broken, leave a threshed-out matter in worse shape than it was to begin with.

"I suggest," I told him, "that you are too squeamish to find and bring out of your unconscious Lovey Mine."

"I have never known a Lovey Mine," he lied.

"Yes, you have," I insisted. "She is the cuddly girl that you and I, when we were in our early teens, wanted to make comfy cozy, and you damn well know why."

"I do *not* know why," snapped Dr. Winterhorn. "I shall ask you to refrain from putting desires in my libido." He was beginning to slip, all right.

"The reason we wanted to make her comfy cozy," I said, "is that we loved her from head to toesy."

A glint came into Dr. Winterhorn's eyes and he stood up again. "I suggest that your favorite old ballad," he said, "is 'Slumber On, My Little Gypsy Sweetheart.' Now, why do you want her to slumber on? Why do you not have an

104

ardent desire to wake her up, since you are obviously alone with her in whatever room she is slumbering in?"

"Careful, Doctor," I warned him. "You are about to expose your own inner conflicts and, if I may say so, sexual disturbances."

"You may *not* say so!" he roared.

"Gypsy sweethearts do not sleep in rooms," I explained, "but in God's great outdoors, with all the other gypsies standing around, potential voyeurs."

"Defense mechanism!" the doctor barked. I lit a cigarette with a slow-motion deliberation that I knew would irritate him and said, "You were thinking of 'Beautiful Dreamer, Wake Unto Me.' " I blew a lazy smoke ring, and added, "Lay off my beautiful dreamer, Snooky Ookums."

At this point my wife hurried over to our corner to break it up. "I shall not desist from further exploration of your husband's confused psyche," Dr. Winterhorn said angrily, but unevenly. Since my wife soon saw that she could not break it up, she brought over a pretty girl and planted her between us. "I wanna sing," the newcomer murmured. "Nobody loves me, I wonder who," she crooned drowsily. The doctor glowered at her. "Let our host sing," he said firmly. "He is a prisoner of the patterns of the past. Music and lyrics have changed with the march of time, but he still wants a girl just like the girl that married dear old Dad." He ended with a triumphant, almost wicked smile, and I heard my wife take in a quick, apprehensive breath.

She knew what was coming (she had heard it a hundred times in recent months), and it came. I clearly proved to my now distraught guest that I have kept pace with the music and the lyrics, the violence, and the horror humor of our decade, for I sang: "I want a ghoul just like the ghoul that buried dead old Dad." And then I went on to disfigure, in the modern manner, another old tender love ballad: "I Wonder Who's Killing Her Now."

The pretty young lady dropped her half-emptied glass on the floor. "I saw that on television last week," she said. "It was perfectly wonderful." Dr. Winterhorn stalked away from us, grabbed the wrong hat in the hall, got in his car, and drove angrily away.

My wife had the last word. "Well, I'll say one thing for you," she remarked. "When you throw a party, it *always* hits *some*body."

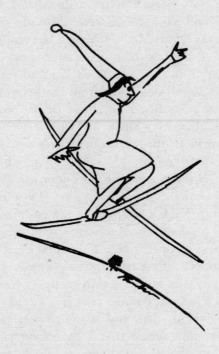

14

Brother Endicott

ꙮꙮꙮꙮꙮꙮꙮꙮꙮꙮꙮꙮꙮꙮꙮꙮ

The man stared at the paper in his typewriter with the bleak look of a rain-soaked spectator at a dull football game, and then ripped it out of the machine. He lit a cigarette, put another sheet of paper in the wringer, and began a letter to his publisher, without salutation: "Why you imbeciles have to have a manuscript three months ahead of publication is, by god—" And out came that sheet. Somewhere a clock began striking three, but it was drowned out by a sudden upsurge of Paris night noises.

The street noises of Paris, staccato, profundo, momentary and prolonged, go on all through the summer night, as if hostile hosts were fiercely taking, losing, and regaining desperately disputed corners, especially the bloody angle of the Rue de Rivoli and the Rue de Castiglione, just beneath the windows of the writer's hotel room. Presently he heard the jubilant coming of the Americans, late but indomitable, sleepless but ever fresh, moving in, like the taxis of the Marne, from the Right Bank and the Left, shouting, laughing, amiably cursing, as they enveloped and captured the lobby of the hotel. They loudly occupied corridors and rooms, leaving the King's English sprawled and bleeding on the barricades of night. A detachment of foot cavalry trooped past the writer's door, one of the men singing "Louise" in a bad imitation of Chevalier.

American reinforcements kept on arriving at the hotel, and below his window the writer heard a young feminine voice crying, "For God's sake, Mother, why not? S'only three o'clock!" Her mother's voice cried back at her, "Your father's dead and so am I—that's why not." There was no report from the father, and the writer visualized him lying on the sidewalk, his wallet deflated, a spent and valiant victim of the battle of Paris. The writer emptied a clogged ashtray into a metal wastebasket, switched off the lights in the sitting room of his suite and sprawled on one of the twin beds in the other room. "It may be the Fourth of July to everybody else," he said aloud, as if talking to someone he didn't like, "but it's just two weeks past deadline to me." He turned over the phrase, "The Fourteenth of Deadline," decided there was nothing in it, and was about to take off his right shoe when he heard a knock at the door. He looked at his wristwatch; it was a few minutes past three o'clock.

The late caller was a young woman he had never seen before. She murmured something that sounded like, "My husband—I thought maybe—" and he stood aside to let her in, apologizing for his shirtsleeves. "I was afraid it was the fellas looking for a tenor," he said. "I'm a baritone myself, but out of practice and not in the mood." He put the lights on again in the sitting room, waved casually at a chair and, just as casually, she sat in it. *"Voici le salon,* as they call it," he said. "Makes it sound very proper. What can I do for you? My name's Guy Farland."

"I know," she said. "I've heard you typing at night before. I asked at the desk once, and they said you were here. My name is Marie Endicott."

He reached for his tie and jacket, but she said, with a faint smile, *"Ne vous dérangez pas.* It's too warm."

"Before we get around to your problem," he said, "how about a drink?" He moved to a table containing bottles and glasses and an ice bucket. She nodded when he put his hand on the Scotch bottle. "Not too strong, please," she said. "A lot of soda."

"I mix drinks my own way," he told her, "and I'm said to be good at it. Besides, this is my castle." He took her in as he fixed the highball, figured that she was not more than twenty-three and that she had had quite a few drinks already, rather desperate ones, which she hadn't enjoyed much. He set her drink down on a table beside her chair. "If I were a younger writer I would say, 'She looked like a chic luna moth in her light green evening gown, as she stood there clutching a dainty evening bag.' But you weren't clutching it, just holding it," he said. "And I'm a middle-aged writer, not a young one."

She picked up her drink but didn't taste it. "I've read your *Lost Corner* four times," she said. He went back to mix himself a drink, saying, "It isn't quite that good. I'm trying to finish another book, but you can't think against this goddam racket. I had got used to the Paris taxi horns and their silence makes me edgy. They have cut out the best part of the noise and left in the worst."

"The goddam motorcycles," she said tonelessly. He sat down, and they both listened to the tumult outside the window for a moment. "The noise has loused me up—I choose the precise word for it," he said. "It would certainly rain in Verlaine's heart if he could hear it." She was look-

109

ing at him as though he were an actor in a spotlight, and he responded with performance. "I was thinking how silent Paris must have been the night François Villon vanished into immortality through the snows of yesteryear. If your husband has vanished, maybe I can help you find him. I'm a husband myself, and I know where they go. On the Fourth of July, of course, it's a little harder, especially in a foreign country." He had left the door to the suite ajar, and they could hear a male quartet somewhere down the hall dwelling liquidly on "The Sweetheart of Sigma Chi."

"Edward isn't lost," she said. "He's the bass. Edward Francis Endicott." She seemed to add a trace of bitters to the name. "Wisconsin Alpha. They're in Rip Morgan's room, with a couple of Americans they picked up at this nightclub. Edward and Rip insisted on singing 'On Wisconsin'—I don't know why we weren't put out—and these strange men knew the words and joined in, but they are from Illinois, and so then they all sang 'Loyal to You, Illinois.' Our honeymoon has been like that ever since Edward ran into Rip Morgan in Rome." She gave the word "honeymoon" a tart inflection. The quartet down the hall now had "Dear Old Girl" in full swing, and Farland got up and closed the door. "They sound a little older than juniors or seniors," he said, coming back to his chair. She took a long swallow of her drink and set the glass down.

"Edward will be forty-six next week," she said, in the tone of a patient on a psychiatrist's couch, and Farland leaned back for the flow he felt was coming. "He still wears his fraternity pin. He wore it on his pajamas on our wedding night. It's the Nelson Merit Pin. He got it one year for being biggest Boopa Doopa Chi in the whole damn country. He has a smaller one, too. Fraternity is

110

his life. Maybe you've heard of Endicott Emblems, Incorporated. Well, he's the president. They make fraternity pins, and signet rings, and everything. He goes around all the time, even over here, with his right hand out like this." She separated the thumb and little finger of her right hand from the other fingers. "He gives everybody the grip, in the American Express and at the Embassy, and everywhere he sees an American man. I don't know much about fraternities. I thought it was something men got over, like football practice. I went to Smith."

Farland noticed that she kept glancing over her right shoulder at the door. "Brother Endicott won't break in on us," he said reassuringly. "Quartets never notice that wives are missing. As for my wife, she's in Italy."

"I knew she wasn't here," Marie Endicott said, and Farland followed her gaze about the room, which must have revealed instantly to his visitor the lack of a woman's touch. There were books and papers on the floor, and that unmistakable masculine rearrangement of chairs and lamps which a man finds comfortable and a woman intolerable. "Nancy is going to pick up our daughters in Italy—we have two. They are coming over on one of the Export ships because they wanted to see Gibraltar. I don't work at night when Nancy's here. Wives don't think it's healthy."

"Ellen Morgan went to bed," said the girl, "and Edward thinks I'm in bed, too." She took several long swallows of her drink this time, and sat forward in her chair. "The reason I'm here, the thing is," she began, with a flash of firmness, and then leaned back with a helpless flutter of her left hand. Farland gave her a cigarette and held a match for her.

"Don't get a blockage," he said easily. "I'm the one with the blockage. I was thinking of throwing the heroine of

111

my novel out of a window, but you can't do that in novels, only in real life." The girl wasn't listening.

"Edward can't stand any foreign country," she said, "because it isn't God's country, and they don't use God's money, and you can't get God's martinis, or God's anything." Her eyes drifted toward an unopened bottle of bourbon on the table. "Or God's whiskey," she said. "Bourbon is God's whiskey, you know."

"He must have trouble getting God's ice, too," Farland put in, "especially at this hour."

"They don't supply soap at most French hotels," she went on. "In the hotel in Le Havre he called downstairs and said, 'Some of you cave dwellers come up here with some soap and make it snappy. Endicott wants soap.' He speaks of himself in the third person a lot of the time. He doesn't know any French except *'combien'* and *'trop cher'* and *'encore la même chose'* and *'où est le cabinet?'* He calls terraces sitdowns, and he's terrible about the new franc. He says, *'Pas si* goddam *vite'* to taxi drivers. He learned what he calls doughboy French from his brother Harry. Harry is much older. He was in the First World War. You know doughboy French? *'Restez ici* a minute. *Je retourner après cet* guy *partirs.'* " She drank some more and went back to brother Harry. "Harry thinks he's dying," she said. "He thinks he's dying of everything, but there isn't anything the matter with him. He ought to go to a psychiatrist, and he actually did once, but the doctor said something like, 'If you're not sick, and you think you're sick, you're sick.' And Harry slammed out of his office."

"Nice slamming," Farland said. "I think I would have, too."

The girl in the green dress took in a long sad breath and exhaled slowly. "Harry carries a little mirror, like a woman, and keeps looking at his mouth, even in public," she said. "He thinks there's something the matter with his uvula."

"I'm sorry you told me that," Farland said. "It is the only part of my body I have never been conscious of. Can you die of uvulitis or something?"

"Harry and his wife were over here," the girl continued, "but they flew back last week, thank God. He suddenly got the idea in the middle of the night that his doctor had secretly called Irene and told her he was dying—Harry, I mean. 'This is my last vacation,' he screamed, waking Irene up. She thought he had lost his mind in his sleep. 'I'm not going to die in Naples or any other foreign city!' he yelled. 'I'm going to die in Buffalo!' *We* live in Milwaukee. It isn't far enough from Buffalo."

"You were just about to tell me why you came here. I don't mean to Europe, I mean to my chambers, tonight—this morning," Farland said, but she postponed the reason for her call with a wave of her hand. He sat back and let her flow on. "Edward is a collector," she said. "Big heavy things, like goal posts. He's football crazy, too. I thought he was really crazy once when we were having a cocktail and he lifted his glass and said, 'Here's to Crazy Legs!' That's Roy Hirsch," she explained. "One of the Wisconsin gridiron immortals. He also drinks to the Horse. That's Ameche. He's immortal, too."

"I'm trying to figure out what you saw in Edward Endicott," Farland said, a flick of impatience in his tone. "It's supposed to be a human mystery, I know, but there's usually a clue of some kind."

She gestured with her hand again and frowned. "He has more drums than anybody else in the world," she went on. "He began collecting them when he was a little boy, and

113

now he has African drums and Maori drums and some from the Civil War and one from the Revolution. He even has a drum that was used in the road company of *The Emperor Jones,* and one of the forty or fifty that were used in *Valencia* during a big production number at the Casino de Paris in 1925, I think it was." She shuddered slightly, as if she heard all the Endicott drums approaching. "Is collecting goal posts Freudian?" she asked.

Farland decided to think that over while he freshened the drinks. "I don't think so," he said. "Goal posts are trophies, a sign your side won. The Indians had it worked out better, of course. Scalping the captain of the losing team would be much simpler. Where does he keep the goal posts?"

"In the attic," she said, "except for the one in the guest room. It belonged to Southern Cal. or S.M.U., or somebody we didn't expect to beat and did." She managed a small evil inflection on "we."

"All right, let's have it," Farland said. "Why did you come here tonight? All this is overture, I can tell that."

She sat forward suddenly again. "Tom will be here, I mean right here, in your suite, in a few minutes," she said, hurriedly. "He sent me a message by a waiter at the night-club, while Edward was trying to get the little French orchestra to play 'Back in Your Own Back Yard.' Tom must have followed me there. I had to think quick, and all I could think of was your room, because you're always up late."

Farland got up and put on his tie and coat. "I ought to look more *de rigueur* for Tom," he said. "You're not constructing this very well. You don't just hit your readers with a character named Tom. They have a right to know who he is and what he wants."

"I'm sorry," she said. "I mean about asking him to come
114

here. He's awfully difficult, but at least he isn't predictable. He loves to sweep everything off the mantelpiece when he's mad, but he doesn't use a straight razor and strop it all the time, like Edward. Tom and I were engaged for years, but he didn't want to get married until he got through his army service, so we broke up about that. Everybody else got married and went to camp with their husbands. They had four million babies last year, the American girls."

"American girls often marry someone they can't stand to spite someone they can," he said. "That's a pretty rough generalization, but I haven't got time to polish it up. Is that where Brother Endicott came in?"

"I don't really know what state Tom is in," she said. "He just got out of the service, and I was afraid he would follow me here. It's a long story about how I met Edward. I wanted to come back to Paris. You see, I had spent my junior year here, and I loved Paris. Of course, my mother went completely to pieces. I had a job in New York, but every evening when I got home Mother was waiting for me. Sometimes crocked. She always wanted to have a little talk. We had more little talks than all the mothers and daughters in the world. I was going crazy, and then I met Edward. He seemed so strong and silent and—" She groped for a word and came up with "attentive." Farland give her another cigarette. "He wasn't really strong and silent. He was just on the wagon. Tom hadn't written for months, and I thought maybe he had another girl, and Edward promised to bring me to Paris, and so—I don't know."

"Paris seems to be full of American girls who are hiding out from their mothers," Farland said. This caused a flash of lightning in her eyes.

"Mother belongs to the damn lost generation," she said.

115

"The trouble with the lost generation is it didn't get lost enough. All the damn lost mothers had only one child," she went on, warming to what was apparently a familiar thesis. "They all think their daughters are weak enough to do the things they thought they were strong enough to do. So we have to pay for what they did. I'm glad I missed the 1920's. God."

"They've stopped singing," Farland said. "They must be taking a whiskey break. How do I fit into this—for Tom, I mean? I don't want to be knocked cold when he gets here. I seem to be in the middle."

As if it were an entrance cue, there were two sharp raps on the door. Farland hurried out and opened it. A tall young man breezed past him and into the sitting room. "Are you all right?" he demanded of the girl.

"No," Farland said. "Do you want a drink?"

"This is Mr. Farland, Mr. Gregg," said Mrs. Endicott. Mr. Gregg scowled at his host. "I don't get this," he said. "What is that baboon doing now? Could I have a straight Scotch?" Farland put some Scotch and ice in a glass and gave it to him.

"They're probably running out of whiskey," the girl said. "I don't want Edward to find me gone."

"He might as well get used to it," said Tom. He began pacing. "I was hanging around out front when you left the hotel," he said, "and I followed you to that nightclub. It cost me five bucks for one drink, five bucks and taxi fare to write that note." He suddenly pulled the girl up out of her chair and into his arms.

"This is pretty damned unplanned," Farland said.

"I got to have half an hour with Marie. We've got to settle some things," Tom said peremptorily. "I'm sorry I was so abrupt." He held out the hand that swept things

116

off mantelpieces. He had a quick, firm grip. "I haven't got any plans, except to get her away from that monkey," he said.

"The law is on his side, of course," Farland put in, "and the church and all that sort of thing." The girl had freed herself and sat down again, and Tom resumed his pacing.

"Do you know the grip?" Farland asked her suddenly. "I think it may be mine. Don't hit me," he said to the young man.

"Tom threw his pledge pin across the room at a chapter meeting, I think they call it," the girl said.

"Somebody said something," Tom snarled.

Farland nodded. "People have a way of doing that," he said. "Human failing." He held out his right hand to the girl and she gave him the grip. "Now I do *this,*" he said, pressing her wrist. "And I do *this,*" she said, returning the pressure. Each then pressed the other's thumb.

"Don't you wiggle your ears, for crissake?" Tom snarled.

"Brother Endicott," Farland sighed, "shake hands with Brother Farland. Pennsylvania Gamma." He picked up the unopened bottle of bourbon and the ice bucket. "I think I can promise you your half hour undisturbed," he said. "God's whiskey and the grip ought to do it, and besides, I know the words of 'Back in Your Own Back Yard.' I also know the 'Darling' song."

"God," said Marie Endicott.

Tom stopped pacing and looked at Farland. "Damned white of you," he said, "but I don't know why you're doing it."

"Lady in distress," Farland said. "Cry for help in the night. I don't know much about drums, but I can talk about Brother Hunk Elliot."

"Ohio Gamma," said Mrs. Endicott bleakly. "Greatest by God halfback that ever lugged a football, even if he did beat Wisconsin three straight years. Crazy Legs and the Horse don't belong to Boopa Doopa Chi, so they don't rate with Brother Elliot."

"The protocol of fraternity is extremely complicated and uninteresting," Farland said.

"Nuts," snapped Tom, who had begun to crack his knuckles. "Why doesn't that goddam racket stop?" He suddenly leaped at the open window of the salon and shouted into the night, "Cut down that goddam noise!"

"Do you want everybody *in* here?" the girl asked nervously.

"I don't see why I shouldn't go down there myself and bust him a couple," he said. "I don't see why you had to marry him anyway. Nobody in her right mind would marry a man old enough to be her father, and live in Milwaukee." He whirled and stared at Farland. "I don't see what you're getting out of this," he said, "acting like her fairy godfather or somebody."

"I—" Farland began, but Mrs. Endicott cut in on him.

There was a new storm in her eyes. "He's done more for me in one night than you have in two years!" she said. "You never wrote, and when you did, nobody could read it, the way you write. How do I know who you were running around with in Tacoma? You're not really in love with me, you just want something somebody else has got." Farland tried to get in on it again, but Tom Gregg gave him a little push and turned to the girl again.

"It wasn't Tacoma," he said. "You didn't even bother to find out what camp I was at."

"Seattle, then," she said. "Fort Lawton. And everybody else got married. I know ten girls who went to camp with their husbands, and three of them were in Tacoma."

"We couldn't get married on nothing," he said. "I happen to have a job now, a good job."

"Everybody else got married on nothing," she said.

"I'm not everybody else!" he yelled. "I'm not just anybody else, either. 'Miss Withrow, I want you to meet Mr. Endicott.' 'How do you do, Miss Withrow. Will you marry me?' 'Sure, why not? I think I'm engaged to a guy named Tacoma or something, but that's okay.' "

"I'll hit you, I really will!" cried the former Miss Withrow.

Farland hastily put the bottle and the ice bucket on the floor and stepped between them. "I'm not anybody's fairy godfather," he said. "I'm just an innocent bystander. I was about to go to bed when all this hell broke loose, and I'll be damned if I'm going down to that room and sing with a lot of big fat emblem makers if you're going to spend your time fighting." His voice was pitched even louder than theirs. The telephone rang. Farland picked up the receiver and listened for three seconds to a voice on the other end speaking in French. "It's the Fourth of July!" he

119

yelled, and slammed down the receiver.

"I'm sorry about this," Tom said. "I'm willing to talk it over rationally if she is. I got to fly back to work day after tomorrow."

"Oh, sure," said Marie.

"I don't usually lose my temper," Farland apologized, "but I'm stuck in a book I'm writing, and it makes me jumpy." He picked up the bottle and the ice bucket again. "I'll give you until four o'clock," he said. "I'll knock four times, with an interval after the third."

"You probably haven't got your key," Marie said. She spied it, put it in Farland's pocket, and kissed him on the forehead.

"Do you have to keep doing that?" Tom shouted.

"I haven't *been* doing that," Marie said.

"Please!" Farland said. "I'm tossing her aside like a broken doll, anyway." He grinned. "How in hell can I open this door with my arms loaded?" Marie crossed over and opened the door for him. "For God's sake, don't kiss me again," he whispered, "and stop fighting and get something worked out." He raised his voice and spoke to both of them. "Goodnight," he said, "and shut up." He stepped out into the hall and the girl in the green dress quietly closed the door after him. . . .

A short, heavy-set man in his middle forties opened the door, and seemed to block the way aggressively until he caught sight of the American face of the visitor and the things he was carrying. "I heard the Yankee Doodle sounds," Farland told him, and introduced himself. "I thought maybe you needed reinforcements." The room exploded into American sounds, as if the newcomer had dropped a lighted match in a box of fireworks. Somebody
120

took the bourbon from him and somebody else the ice bucket. "My God, it's real ice!" someone said, and "Brother, you've saved our lives!"

"An American shouldn't spend this night alone," Farland said above the hubbub. The biggest man in the room, who wore no coat or tie, but on whose vest a fraternity pin gleamed, held out his hand in three parts. Farland gave him the full-dress grip. "Ed Endicott, Wisconsin Alpha!" bawled the big man.

"Pennsylvania Gamma," Farland said.

"For crissake, it's a small world!" Endicott said. "Rip, shake hands with Brother Farland, give him the old grip. Brother Morgan and I belong to the same chapter. Wisconsin Alpha has two national presidents to its credit," he told Farland, "and I was one of them, if I do say so myself. These other poor guys took the wrong pins, but they're okay." He managed somehow to get his right arm around the shoulders of both the other men in the room. "This is Sam Winterhorn, Phi Gam from Illinois, and this is Red Perry, also Illini—Red's a Phi Psi. Maybe you heard us doing 'Fiji Honeymoon' and 'When DKE Has Gone to Hell.' Put 'er there again, fella."

Farland was glad when he was finally given a glass to hold instead of a man's right hand. "Here's to all the brothers, whatever sky's above 'em," Endicott said, clinking his glass against Farland's. He took a great gulp of his drink, and it seemed to Farland that his face brightened like a full moon coming out from behind a cloud. "Endicott is a curly wolf this night, Guy, and you can write that home to your loved ones!" he roared. "Endicott is going to shake hands with the pearly-fingered dawn this day. Endicott is going to ring all the bells and blow all the whistles in hell. Any frog that don't like it can bury his head in the

Tooleties." Farland managed to get out part of a word, but Brother Endicott trampled on it. "The girls have gone to bed," he said. "Wish you could meet Marie, but we'll be around a couple of more days. Marie's Eastern women's college, but Brenda—that's my first wife—was a Kappa. So's Ellen Morgan, Rip's wife. Brenda hated drums. I got the greatest little drum collection in the world, Guy. Once, when a gang of us got up a storm in my house—this was six-seven years ago—damned if Brenda didn't call the cops! One of them turned out to be real mean with the sticks, but the other guy was a surly bastard. I tried to give him the grip, and he got sore as hell. Don't ever try to give a cop the grip, Guy. They think you're queer. Sons-of-bitches never get through high school."

Farland put on his fixed grin as Endicott rambled on, moving among the disarranged chairs like a truck. He paused in front of one in which Brother Morgan now lay back relaxed, with his eyes closed. "Judas Priest, our tenor's conking out," he said.

" 'Way," mumbled Morgan sleepily.

"Let him sleep," said the man named Perry. "What the hell, we still got a quartet. Anyway, what good's a sleepy tenor unless you're doing 'Sleepy Time Gal'?"

" 'Sleepy Time Gal!' " bawled Endicott, and he suddenly started in the middle of the old song, biting a great hunk out of the lyric. The phone rang, and Endicott smote the night with a bathroom word and jerked up the receiver. "Yeah?" he began truculently, and, as the voice at the other end began protesting in French, he said to the revellers, "It's one of them quoi-quois." He winked heavily at Farland and addressed the transmitter. *"Parlez-vous la langue de Dieu?"* he asked. Farland realized he had been rehearsing the question quite a while. *"Bien,* then," Endicott went

122

on. "You people ought to be celebrating, too. If we hadn't let Lafayette fight on our side, he would have gone to the goddam guillotine. The way it was, even Napoleon didn't dare lay a hand on him. They cut the head off Rabelais and Danton, but they couldn't touch Lafayette, and that's on account of the good old Thirteen States." The person at the other end had apparently hung up, but Endicott went on with his act. "Get yourselves a bottle of grenadine and a pack of cubebs and raise a little hell for Lafayette," he said, and hung up.

"Not Rabelais," Farland couldn't help saying. "Robespierre."

"Or old Roquefort!" Endicott bawled. "They all sound like cheese to me, rich old framboise, and they all look alike. Let's hit the 'Darling' song again."

They got through "Three O'Clock in the Morning" and "Linger Awhile" and "Over There" and "Yankee Doodle Dandy" and "You're the 'B-E-S-T Best" and by that time it was ten minutes after four. "Don't keep looking at your Benrus," Endicott told Farland. "Nobody's going anywhere. What the hell, we've got all day." Rip Morgan's troubled unconscious greeted this with a faint moaning sound. Farland's tone grew firm and terminal, and the Illinois men joined him and began the final round of handshakes. Farland picked up the ice bucket, which had been empty for some time now, and started for the door.

"We'll all meet in the bar downstairs at six," Endicott commanded. "Be there!" The two departing Americans said they would be there. "I'm going to stay stiff till they pour me on the plane," Endicott went on. Farland's hand felt full of fingers after he had shaken hands again with the Illinois men and they had gone. Brother Endicott, he felt sure, would have his hands full for at least fifteen

123

minutes, putting Brother Morgan to bed. . . .

Farland rapped on the door of his suite three times, paused, and rapped again. There was no response, and he unlocked the door and went in. All the lights in the sitting room were out except one, and he turned it off and began undressing before he reached the bedroom. The battle of the Paris night still went on, and it seemed louder than ever. Farland put on the bottom of his pajamas, couldn't find the top, said, "The hell with it," and went into the bathroom and brushed his teeth. "Everything happens to you," he sneered at the man in the mirror. "What's the matter, don't you know how to duck any more?"

He was about to throw himself on his bed when he noticed the note on his pillow. It read simply, "You are the B-E-S-T Best," and it was signed, obviously in Mrs. Endicott's handwriting, "Tom and Marie." In spite of the noise and his still tingling right hand, Farland fell asleep. When he woke up, he picked up the telephone and called the *renseignement* desk. He looked at his watch. It was nine-thirty-five. "I want to get a plane out of here for Rome this afternoon," he said when the information desk answered. "A single seat. And I don't care what line. There is just one thing. It has *got* to leave before six o'clock."

15

The Manic in the Moon

ㅎㅎㅎㅎㅎㅎㅎㅎㅎㅎㅎㅎㅎㅎㅎㅎㅎㅎㅎㅎㅎㅎㅎ

"Most trains of thought and avenues of conversation lead eventually to the moon nowadays," a professor observed at a summer party in Connecticut. We had been talking about President Kennedy's gift to Khrushchev in Vienna of a replica of the frigate Constitution, and my companion wondered how many young Americans know that the Constitution was Old Ironsides. At this moment, we were joined by a young female American who said she didn't know, and couldn't care less. I asked her if she had never heard of the line "Old Ironsides at anchor lay in the harbor of Mahon."

"No," she said, "and I don't want to know where Mahon is, if there *is* a Mahon." She left us abruptly for the company of less disturbed persons, and the professor said, "It would have been a clever piece of propaganda if the President had had a paraphrase of that line engraved in tiny words on the prow of the frigate: 'Old Ironsides at anchor lay in the harbor of the moon.'"

Since we were now launched successfully into space, we went on to discuss the letters published in *Izvestia* from

125

formerly religious readers who had suddenly given up their belief in God because of the flights of Gagarin and Titov. One of these correspondents, I have been told, said that this minute monkeying around in a minuscule corner of the universe (that is my own description of it) proved that science is God, and only Man is truly super and supernal. Why this person had not been saved by the new scientific salvation when the eight-engine bomber was invented, or the H-bomb, I do not know. I don't happen to be a phrenetically religious man myself, but I flatly refuse to accept Gagarin as the Son of a new God. Since the professor had got into paraphrase, I suggested that radio would overlook a good bet if it did not revive the old *Superman* series and change the line "It's a bird! It's a plane! It's Superman!" to "It's a bird! It's a plane! It's God!"

To get off the subject of outer space, I remarked that I had had a dream in which the Jehovah of the Old Testament offered me the opportunity of changing species and asked me what species I would choose. I said that I would like to be a warbler, but I couldn't stand the hours.

Charles Wertenbaker (to get back to the moon by a special avenue) coined the paraphrase "Lo, the poor idiom." He couldn't have realized that he was dealing in terms of prophecy, since he died before his restless species began taking competitively to outer space in order to explore the neighborhood of what Alfred North Whitehead called "a second-rate planet with a second-rate sun," thus wryly summarizing the Man-shaking discovery of Copernicus that the earth is not the center of the universe. We all know how Man loves to be the center of everything, from attention to eternity. What is going on now, or going up, would not surprise Whitehead, who would have been over a hundred this year if he had lived. Man has reached both poles, the top of Everest, the bottom of the ocean, and the end of his mundane tether, and there is no place left for him to go but up.

The poor idiom now stands in danger of being turned inside out and upside down as the result of our compulsion to reach the moon and points beyond. It seems certain that many old familiar expressions and solid clichés will undergo, before long, a complete change in meaning and application. Many phrases connoting soundness and security will, it seems to me, become old-fashioned and even obsolete. "Both feet on the ground" will no longer indicate, as the century flies on and up, sanity in a man but cowardice, or, at best, apathy. The same will be true of "down to earth," "well-grounded," "stands his ground," and "it suits me down to the ground." Conversely, such common usages as "up in the air" and "going around in circles" and "looping" must lose their sense of flightiness and become symbols of flight. These prospective reversals of meaning are likely to contribute to what is already being called the "space neurosis." "The world is too much with us" will not be easy to explain, in a decade or so, to a foreigner striving to learn and make sense out of the New English.

One of the inevitable changes that I view with alarm will be in the area of phrases now associated with nobility of character, gallantry, and beauty. Medical science will not be able to determine for many years, I understand, the effects of space travel on the human mind and organism—effects that may be grave and, for all anybody knows, fatal. Thus, "light-hearted" may come to mean a cardiac condition, and "high-minded" may be solely applied to mental states brought about by speed, momentum, and distance from the earth. I deplore the possibility that "earth goddess" may come to signify a female human being

127

unwilling to accompany her husband into the wild blue yonder, hence maladjusted, behind the times, timorous, and even psychotic. Such a woman will not be, alas, "out of this world." I shudder to think that "starry-eyed" may no longer describe a pretty girl, aglow with love, hope, and wonder, but an ophthalmological ailment similar to glaucoma. And let us pray that "out of sight, out of mind" will not mean, in the interstellar future, temporarily blinded and demented by soaring too close to the sun.

I can foresee in, say, the year 2000 the kind of phrases the disgruntled wife of an inveterate space traveller will

hurl at her husband after he has been rocketing around in the empyrean off and on for a decade or so. I have a premonition that they will include "Go jump into space," "Tell it to the Martians!," "Get lost in the stars," and "I'm tired of you throwing your weightlessness around."

An American friend of mine in London, where I recently spent several months trying not to think about the future, staggered into my hotel room one day, asked me for God's sake to give him a drink, and, when I did, began pouring out his fears about the coming ominous effects of space mania upon certain popular songs in which the moon figures as a romantic symbol of love and lovers. "We can't keep on singing 'The moon belongs to everyone, the best things in life are free,'" he babbled, "if either Russia or the United States plants its flag on the moon first." What especially worried my friend, he told me on his second drink, was what will happen to the last line of the old ballad called "I'll Be Seeing You." I didn't happen to remember that last line offhand, and so he sang it for me: "I'll be looking at the moon, but I'll be seeing you." He sang it so loudly and with such a note of terror in his voice that my wife rushed in from the next room and said, "Are you all right?" We both said "No," in unison, and she withdrew and shut the door behind her. "The women are not worrying enough," my friend said.

"They're down to earth, that's why," I told him. "They have a leg to stand on." And then I asked, "What worries you so much about that last line you just sang?"

"I'll tell you what worries me about it," he said. "I woke up this morning and found myself singing 'I'll be looking at the moon, but I'll be seeing U.S.S.R.' Then I got into 'I've told every little star just how wonderful U.S.S.R.'" He sat down and put his head in his trembling hands.

"You're going to get the Birch Society after you if you don't look out," I warned him. "If you're going to go air-minded—that is, space-kooky—for heaven's sake do it patriotically."

"How?" he demanded.

"Well," I said, "take that old Crosby ballad 'Moonlight Becomes You.' Now, the last line of that goes 'Moonlight becomes you so.' Why not change that to 'Moonlight becomes U.S.'? You might also try 'I told every milky way all about the U.S.A.'"

My moon-struck visitor wasn't listening, though, and suddenly began walking up and down again. "How do we know stars fell on Alabama?" he demanded. "Maybe they were thrown there—by a Castronaut!" he yelped. He walked over and waved a finger at me, as if I were to blame for it all: "Do you know what moonbeams will become?" he said. "They will become messages beamed at the moon! Even if the moon finally does belong to us, it will no longer be one of the best things in life that are free. It will cost forty-eight billion dollars."

"Nobody has planted a flag on the moon yet," I reminded him. "It still has its place in poetry and romance, and, as a satellite, it still goes on affecting the tides."

"It affects the tides and the fit-to-be-tieds," my friend said mournfully.

Before long, he went to sleep in his chair, and for a while I sat brooding about the imminent disfigurations of sense and meaning. "Inner man" would someday be nothing more than a man inside a space capsule, and "somebody up there loves me" would be an allusion to a husband, lover, father, or son in orbit.

I went into the bedroom and asked my wife what we should do about my visitor. "Why don't you call his wife and tell her to come over and get him?" she said. So I telephoned his flat, but his wife was out, and Clara, the maid, answered the phone. Clara is a foreigner who has always spoken an unknown language all her own, but I discovered, to my dismay, that it had become distorted by my space thoughts.

"She has gone to the moonies," said Clara, "I mean the movies. Now wasn't that stupnik of me!"

"Get thee to a moonery," I said, and hung up on her.

"What's the matter with everybody?" my wife asked, meaning me, my space-ridden friend in the next room, and all other men. I thought it over for a moment and then told her.

"Everybody is talking in moon syllables," I said. "It's becoming moonotonous. It's a goddam moonstrosity." I thought that covered it, but my wife, as she so often does, topped me.

"You're moondoggling," she said. "Why don't you get your mind on something else?"

When I went back into the living room, my friend was wide awake again and fixing himself a double Scotch and soda. He took up his babbling where he had left off. "In ten years everything we now say will have a new meaning, or maybe I should say a new mooning."

"Please don't," I broke in, but he went right on.

"Footloose and fancy free will become footloose and fanny free, meaning the astronaut can't get his feet on the floor of the spaceship or his bottom on the chair. A fast woman will simply be one who is going at a speed of seventeen hundred miles a minute. If she is in a delicate condition, it will mean she is so far from earth that she weighs less than fifteen pounds."

I got him to his flat in Russell Square somehow, and

131

turned him over to his wife, who had got back from the moonies. When she had put him to bed and returned to the living room, she pointed nervously at a potted plant on a table. "Do you know what he calls that?" she quavered.

"I can guess," I said. "He calls it a potted planet." I was right.

"When I got home, I found Clara in tears," she told me. "She said you told her to get her to a moonastery."

"I did not," I said. "I would never tell a woman to get her to a moonastery. *You* know that."

"I don't know what I know. I don't know what anybody is talking about any more."

My hotel in London is near Green Park, and when I am there in spring and summer I am waked each morning by the gay singing of a blackbird. His song takes my mind off the moony present and the star-crossed future, and back to the tranquil years that W. E. Henley wrote about. The morning after my friend's descent upon me, I began whistling in bed, accompanied by the blackbird's boxwood flute. This woke up my wife, who said drowsily, "I'm glad you're in a better moon—I mean—"

"I know what you mean," I told her, "but for God's sake don't tell me I'm in high spirits. High spirits is what you drink from a flask when you are two hundred and fifty thousand miles from earth."

"It isn't far enough," my wife murmured as she dropped off to sleep again. I wasn't so lucky.

When I got back to my home in the United States, I turned to the Oxford English Dictionary and looked up "moon." One of the definitions I encountered was "moonproof: proof against the moon's light or influence." Obviously, we are going to need moon-proofers as time goes onward and upward. The practice of moon-proofing may

132

even become a branch of psychiatry, like psychotherapy. The expression "in a moon" once meant "in a fit of frenzy," and the moon-proofers will have to get their patients out of that condition.

Paul Nash, the English painter and critic, who died long before the race into space began, once did a collage showing the moon being attacked by a certain European herb with showy flowers, and he called his creation "Last Night Light and Heavy Hellebores Bombed the Mountains of the Moon." I found, on looking up the herb in the dictionary, that the powdered root of the white American hellebore is used to kill lice and caterpillars. Now, it happens that lice and caterpillars are not two of my many problems, but I keep thinking about Paul Nash's floral bombers, and I wish he were still on earth to do another, more timely collage, one to be entitled "Last Night Light and Heavy Moonbores Attacked the Mountains of the Earth."

What do you say we all sleep outdoors one of these balmy summer nights, braving the agitating effects of moonlight? We might even try to remember the years when tranquillity did not come in bottles but was a simple anodyne of nature, the years when the outdoors at night, under the light of our so disturbing satellite, was serenely known as the Inn of the Silver Moon.

16

E. B. W.

ᴕᴕᴕᴕᴕᴕᴕᴕᴕᴕᴕᴕᴕᴕᴕᴕᴕᴕᴕ

Once, a few years ago, a gentleman came to the offices of *The New Yorker* and asked for E. B. White. He was shown into the reception room and Mr. White was told that someone was waiting for him there. White's customary practice in those days, if he couldn't place a caller's name, was to slip moodily out of the building by way of the fire escape and hide in the coolness of Schrafft's until the visitor went away. He is not afraid of process servers, blackmailers, borrowers, or cranks; he is afraid of the smiling stranger who tramples the inviolable flowers of your privacy bearing a letter of introduction from an old Phi Gam brother now in the real estate game in Duluth. White knows that the man in the Reception Room may not be so easy to get rid of as a process server—or even a blackmailer; he may grab great handfuls of your fairest hours, he may even appropriate a sizable chunk of your life, for no better reason than that he was anchor man on your brother's high school relay team, or married the sister of your old girl, or met an aunt of yours on a West Indies cruise. Most of us, out of a politeness made up of faint curiosity and profound resignation, go out to meet the smiling stranger with a

134

gesture of surrender and a fixed grin, but White has always taken to the fire escape. He has avoided the Man in the Reception Room as he has avoided the interviewer, the photographer, the microphone, the rostrum, the literary tea, and the Stork Club. His life is his own. He is the only writer of prominence I know of who could walk through the Algonquin lobby or between the tables at Jack and Charlie's and be recognized only by his friends.

But to get back to the particular caller whom we left waiting in the reception room. On that occasion, out of some obscure compulsion, White decided to go out and confront the man and see what he wanted. "I'm White," he told the stranger he found sitting alone in the room. The man rose, stared for a long moment at the audacious fellow in front of him, and then said, with grim certainty, "You are not E. B. White." White admits that his hair leaped up, but it is my fond contention that his heart did, too. I like to think that he was a little disappointed when he realized, as he was bound to, that the man was wrong. I like to insist that he resumed his burden of identity with a small sigh. (Where the remarkable interview got to from the tense point to which I have brought it here I shall leave it to my memoirs to tell.)

In the early days of *The New Yorker* the object of this searching examination signed his first few stories and poems with his full name: Elwyn (as God is my judge) Brooks White. I cannot imagine what spark of abandon, what youthful spirit of devil-may-care prompted a poet who loves to live half-hidden from the eye to come out thus boldly into the open. He didn't keep it up long; he couldn't stand that fierce glare of polysyllabic self-acknowledgment. For some years now he has signed his casuals and his verses merely with his initials, E. B. W. To his friends he is Andy.

It was a lucky break that saved him from Elly or Wynnie or whatever else one might make out of Elwyn in the diminutive. He went to Cornell, and it seems that every White who goes there is nicknamed Andy for the simple if rather faraway reason that the first president of the University was named Andrew White.

It used to be a wonder and a worry to White's boss, Mr. Harold Ross, the mystic and wonderful editor of *The New Yorker*, that his favorite and most invaluable assistant avoided people, lived along the untrodden ways, hid by mossy stones, and behaved generally in what Ross was pleased to call an antisocial manner. For a restlessly gregarious man who consorted with ten thousand people from Groucho Marx to Lord Dalhousie it was difficult to comprehend the spirit of Walden Pond. As long ago as the late 1920's there were hundreds of people who implored Ross to introduce them to the man who wrote, on the already famous first page of *The New Yorker,* those silver and crystal sentences which had a ring like the ring of nobody else's sentences in the world. White declined to be taken to literary parties, or to any other kind of parties, but one day Ross lured him to the house of a certain literary lady who, White was persuaded to believe, would be found alone. When the door of her house was opened to them, Ross pushed White into a hallway loud with the chatter of voices proceeding from a crowded living room, the unmistakably assertive voices of writers and artists. Ross made the serious mistake of entering the living room first. When he looked around for White, that shy young man had quietly disappeared. He had proceeded deviously through the house, to the disciplined dismay of the servants, out the back door, and over trees and fences, or whatever else may have been in his way, to the freedom he so greatly cherishes,

136

leaving the curtsy, the compliment, and the booksy chat to writers who go in for that sort of thing.

"Isn't there," Ross demanded of him one time, "*any*body you would like to meet?" White gave this difficult question his grave consideration and said, at long last, "Yes. Willie Stevens and Helen Hayes." It is a proof of the reckless zeal and the devoted energy of Harold Ross that he instantly set about trying to get hold of Willie Stevens for the purpose of inviting him to a dinner in New York at which White and Miss Hayes were to be the only other guests. I am desolated to report that this little coming together could not be accomplished: Willie apparently knew too many people the way it was and declined the invitation with that gentle old-world courtesy of which he was so consummate a master. Ross did manage finally to bring White face to face with Helen Hayes. Our hero, I am informed, was discontented and tongue-tied during their brief, jumpy conversation and was glad when it was all over. I suppose Miss Hayes was, too.

E. B. W. was born in Mount Vernon, N. Y. He had an ordinary, normal childhood, monkeying with an old Oliver typewriter, shooting with an air gun at the weather vane on his father's barn. At Cornell he charmed and astonished his English professors with a prose style so far above Cayuga's ordinary run of literary talent as to be considered something of a miracle. The *Cornell Sun* under White's editorship must have been the best-written college newspaper in the country. After Cornell he drove a model T Ford across the country with a friend named Howard Cushman. When they ran out of money, they played for their supper—and their gasoline—on a fascinating musical instrument that White had made out of some pieces of wire and an old shoe or something. In Seattle the young explorer got a job as reporter on the *Times,* the kind of newspaper that did not allow you to use the verb "to mangle." Accurately reporting, one day, the anguished cry of a poor husband who had found the body of his wife in the municipal morgue, White wrote "My God, it's her!" and when the city editor changed this to "My God, it is she!" our wanderer moved sadly on to where they had a better understanding of people and a proper feeling for the finer usages of the English tongue. He became mess boy on a ship bound for Alaska, commanded by an old whaling captain, and manned by a crew who knew that a man says it's her when he finds her dead.

Shortly after *The New Yorker* was founded, its editors began to get occasionally manuscripts from an unknown young man named E. B. White who was a production assistant in an advertising agency. Harold Ross and Katharine Angell, his literary editor, were not slow to perceive that here were the perfect eye and ear, the authentic voice and accent for their struggling magazine. It took months, however, to trap the elusive writer into a conference and weeks to persuade him to come to work in the office; he finally agreed to give them his Thursdays. It is not too much to say that Andy White was the most valuable person on the magazine. His delicate tinkering with the works of *The New Yorker* caused it to move with a new ease and grace. His tag lines for those little newsbreaks which the magazine uses at the bottom of columns were soon being read joyfully aloud around town. His contributions to the Talk of the Town, particularly his Notes and Comment on the first page, struck the shining note that Ross had dreamed of striking. He has written a great many of the most memorable picture captions, including the famous one that has passed (usually misquoted) into song and legend, editorial and, I daresay, sermon: "I say it's spinach and I say the hell with it." He had a hand in everything: he even painted a cover and wrote a few advertisements. One day he decided that some pencil drawings I had absently made and thrown on the floor should be published in *The New Yorker,* so he picked them up, inked in the lines, and, to the surprise of us all, including Ross, got them published in *The New Yorker.*

Andy White understands begonias and children, canaries and goldfish, dachshunds and Scottish terriers, men and motives. His ear not only notes the louder cosmic rhythms but catches the faintest ticking sounds. He plays a fair ping-pong, a good piano, and a terrible poker (once, holding four natural jacks, he dropped out of the betting under the delusion that there were eight jacks in the deck and all he had was half of them). He has steadfastly refused to learn to play bridge or to take out life insurance. Once he offered an airplane pilot a thousand dollars to take him through a stormy dawn from Roosevelt Field to Chicago because a mysterious phone call had made him believe a friend was in great distress. The pilot had to make a forced landing in Pittsburgh, so that all White had to pay to see for himself that all was quiet along Lake Michigan was eight hundred dollars and his railroad fare from Pittsburgh. When a band of desperadoes stole his Buick sedan out of a quiet Turtle Bay garage and used it in the robbery of an upstate bank, White was suspected by the New York police of being the "brain guy" who devised the operations of a large and dangerous mob. For days detectives shrewdly infested his office, peering under tables, asking questions, staring in suspicious bewilderment at the preposterous array of scrawls, dentist's dates, symbols, phone numbers, photographs, and maps that littered his walls. Eventually they went shrewdly away, but every time I hear the sirens scream, I think they are coming for White. The former suspect is a good man with ax, rifle, and canoe (for several years he was part owner of a boys' camp in darkest Canada), and he sails a thirty-foot boat expertly. Two of his favorite books are *Van Zanten's Happy Days* and Alain-Fournier's *The Wanderer*. In the country he is afflicted with hay fever and in the city with a dizziness that resembles ordinary dizziness only as the mist resembles the rain. He expects every day of his life that something will kill him: a bit of mold, a small bug, a piece of huckleberry pie.

Some years ago White bought a farm in Maine and he now lives there the year around with his wife, who was Katharine Angell. He spends most of his time delousing turkeys, gathering bantam eggs, building mice-proof closets, and ripping out old fireplaces and putting in new

140

ones. There is in him not a little of the spirit of Thoreau, who believed "that the world crowds round the individual, leaving him no vista, and shuts out the beauty of the earth; and that the wholesome wants of man are few." Now and then, between sunup and milking time, Andy White manages to do a casual or a poem for *The New Yorker*, or write a book. Many of the things he writes seem to me as lovely as a tree—say a maple after the first frost, or the cherry hung with snow. What he will go on to do I have no idea. If he simply continues to do what he has always done, it will be all right with me.

October 15, 1938

17

The Real Man, Nugent

ʊʊʊʊʊʊʊʊʊʊʊʊʊʊʊʊʊʊʊʊʊʊʊʊʊʊʊʊʊʊ

"Isn't Elliott Nugent in real life just exactly like Professor Tommy Turner in *The Male Animal*?" pretty girls squeal at me as they cluster charmingly about my feet at teatime like a tangle of water lilies. To these excited queries I always reply, with simple authority, "No." Elliott Nugent, a timid fellow, a waverer, a man of delicate will, who doesn't know his own mind and cannot read the hearts of others? Perish, my little darlings, the thought!

When Elliott John (for his gifted pappy) was only eight (I have this story from an aunt of his), one of the cuter seven-year-old girls in Dover, Ohio, where Elliott lived, sent him a note in which she confessed that, so great was her love for him, she did not care to go on facing life unless she could face it at his side. Did Elliott act with the indecision of a youthful Tommy Turner, making moan and crying out, "Oh, woe is irreparably me"? He did not. He seized a pencil, wrote firmly across the face of the note the one word "Sorry," and had Jupiter, the old Nugent family retainer, return it to the pining maiden. (Over the fate of the ardent lassie history has mercifully drawn a veil, but it is my guess that she probably lived to work her sweet designs on a man of softer sentiments and a less stern resolve.)

When Nugent comes into a room he comes in to get something; when he gets up from a chair he gets up to do something: read a water meter, change a fuse, develop a film, open a checking account, or look up a number in the phone book (probably for the purpose of telling an equivocator to stop equivocating, or a laggard to quit lagging). On rainy days he writes sonnets, sings little German songs, or plays Mouse, Mouse, Come Out of Your House with his youngest daughter (he has three).

At Ohio State University Elliott was president of the junior class, president of Strollers, vice president of Sphinx, secretary of Bucket and Dipper and chairman of the May Dance Committee. A natural leader of men, this timid professor. During the war he was at Great Lakes Naval Training Center near Chicago, where he was put in charge one night of a dormitory full of tough guys. The man he had succeeded in this job and the man before that man had been unable to get the sailors up in the morning. They just lay in their hammocks and made derisive sounds and wiggled their fingers at their ears, and went back to sleep. On the first morning of Nugent's ordeal he took the center of the floor, struck a posture worthy of James Cagney and bawled out of the corner of his mouth, "Hit the deck, you —— —— ——s!" They hit the deck as one man.

That, my dears, is the real Elliott Nugent. He is older now, of course (although you'd never know it to look at him), and he probably couldn't run the 440 fast enough to tie the State high school record as he did in Ohio in 1915, but he is still a tough hombre when he has to be—I mean if set upon by bandits or pushed into a corner by Ed Kellers or Joe Fergusons.

143

After ten years in Hollywood Nugent can still write clear English sentences, which is to me a wonder unmixed. Hollywood rolled over his even disposition like ducks over a waterfall. His blond head is not only unbowed, it isn't even bloody. He got to be a director by outfoxing and out-gaffing the movie men. He held the sound rights for a certain play for which the movie men held all the other rights. They offered him money, but he didn't want money; he wanted to direct a movie in return for the sound rights. They offered him more money, they offered him polo ponies, pearls, fig newtons, but he was adamant. They cursed and they threatened, but he held out. In the end he wore them down. They let him direct a movie and he went on directing movies, very expertly, for ten years.

His last one, *The Cat and the Canary,* was a big personal triumph for him as director. Its success was so great that the movie men began hauling out all the other old mystery plays of the 1920's in the hope that they could get Nugent to direct them. When he told them that he intended to give up the movies and the movie money to write a play with a tall, nervous man who didn't exactly know what the play was going to be about, they raved and threatened him. When he told them further that he intended to act in the play on Broadway, they howled and screamed. To the movie men actors are Untouchables and a director who becomes one is not only plain nuts but all leprosied over. But Nugent brought his family east, bravely put on grease paint for the first time in ten years, made a few passes in the air, murmured some abracadabra, and, on the opening night, performed the now familiar miracle of coming out on the stage and somehow looking and acting frail and timid and a little sick. His collaborator had meanwhile gone to bed with a high fever and a low blood count.

144

The only disagreeable thing about Nugent is that he is never disagreeable to his friends. There comes a time in your day or your week or your collaboration when, if a person doesn't snarl back when you snarl at him, you feel like going out and throwing stones at wounded lions. This is part of the essential nature of man, but not of Nugent. He only gets mad on the second Sunday in October of the even-numbered years which are divisible by four. At these times he will defy the lightning. You would never believe then that he could assume that death-mask-of-Thomas-Jefferson look which he wears in the play, or speak in that underwater tone of faded perplexity.

His rage raises a lot of hell but abates rapidly, like a sky-rocket shot up the center of the street on a market day. Horrible people crawl back into the woodwork, bullies and bravos slink away, tiger women turn pale, collaborators pipe down. When it is over Elliott goes quietly to sleep, lying without moving on his right side till morning. Occasionally he says something in his sleep. I once came upon him, that little smile on his lips, his eyes closed, saying pleasantly to himself, "Well, well, well." I wondered what it could be that was so pleasant. Me, I am chased by things in my sleep, I can't get my feet out of the sand, doors are locked against me, and the train has pulled out of the station. But Elliott sees the kind of things that make people smile and say, "Well, well, well," as if they were greatly pleased. He got a great many of them into the play.

February, 1940

145

18

The Incomparable Mr. Benchley

One afternoon in 1927 Harold Ross sent me over to the Algonquin to pick up a timely Robert Benchley "casual," or short funny piece, not too much fun to write. This casual was overdue, and Ross was worried. Things had been known to happen to Benchley. Once he was taken unexpectedly to Europe when a ship sailed at midnight while he was seeing friends off in a merry cabin on A deck. "I am very fond of midnight sailings," he once wrote.

On that day in '27, I was a proud young Western Conference spy on *The New Yorker,* and I wouldn't have chased just any Ivy Leaguer's copy, but for Benchley's I would have gone anywhere—to the Harvard Club, if necessary. I read and admired everything he wrote, and I knew how hard it was to do it the way he did it—usually in fewer than fifteen hundred words. He even managed, in the theatre guide of the old *Life*, celebrated masterpieces of from two to fifty words.

I was a little breathless that afternoon so long ago when I first saw Benchley plain. He eased me into a chair, with that warm laugh, and gave me a glass of Moxie. When *The*

New Yorker phoned (for me) he answered, and explained that he was having the devil's own time with a cognate accusative. I had had his copy in my pocket for nearly two hours. It was almost seven o'clock. I had to drag myself away from the enchanting company of my host. This was never, for anybody, an easy thing to do. He was not only the humorist's humorist, he was also their idea of a wonderful guy.

It seemed, as Frank Sullivan says, that everybody wanted to be Bob Benchley's close friend. When he set up, in his suite at the Royalton, the combination men's club, museum, and art gallery that made the hotel famous, it was filled with men who wanted to get his ear, hear his laughter and his talk, and cry on his shoulder. He once had to console a broken-hearted gentleman hopelessly in love with a lady who had been dead a hundred years. He understood Scott Fitzgerald better than anybody else did, when the moon was full and the jugs were out. In one book he tells of a curious experience he had with Hemingway, when Ernie suddenly turned literary vandal and "fixed" Benchley's first editions of Hemingway novels.

Here are some things said about Bob Benchley by a few of his colleagues. Wolcott Gibbs: "People were mysteriously improved in his company, surprisingly at home on a level of easy charm of which nobody would have dreamed they were capable."

Frank Sullivan: "I find myself getting my admiration for Bench's work mixed up with my affection for him. I had a wholesome, benign envy of Bob. I just wished I could be as comical as he was. I also wished I could be the social person he was, sought after by one and all."

E. B. White: "I was always looking for his stuff, and thought he was wonderful, and still think he was wonderful. He was certainly wonderfully kind, and he slayed his dragons with the minimum of pain. He had the gift of brevity, of course, and I was impressed by that, and I'm sure I imitated Benchley and kept trying to do what he was succeeding in doing. The day Ross told me Benchley had praised something I had written was one of the big days of the twenties for me."

Donald Ogden Stewart: "He *was* Humor, with its instinctive humanity, toleration, wisdom, non-competitiveness, non-aggressiveness, democracy (not in the political sense). I warmed myself at that fire and what I wrote always was, unconsciously, for his approval. It still is."

Out of such a personality, lovely stuff was bound to come, but it didn't come easily. The young Benchley had a tough time, as reporter, press agent, editor of a house organ, and miscellaneous drudge. Franklin Pierce Adams, who had gone to Boston in 1915 to bring him to the New York *Tribune,* gave him his first good break, by getting him out of the city room and into Sunday feature work. At the turn of the twenties Benchley hit his stride, and in 1928 he brought out his fifth book of pieces and was the chief reason people bought *Life* in those days. He came to *The New Yorker* as drama critic in 1929.

Benchley's early theatre reviews carried a sword: "We will pause just long enough in front of this exhibit to stick pins in the characters and see if they are alive. Next week the figures will be rearranged to represent the assassination of President McKinley." As he became more and more the actor, and less and less the writer, Benchley was so kind to thespians that they romped boldly in *The New Yorker*'s very parlor until Hollywood claimed him, and the magazine sent for an exterminator named Gibbs. Benchley's "The Wayward Press" and his casuals often had a club handy to the end. For all his kindliness, he could deal a hard blow, and his last *New Yorker* piece (1937) took a slash at Max Eastman's *Enjoyment of Laughter*.

Benchley got off to a fast start ahead of all of us on *The New Yorker*, and our problem was the avoidance of imitation. He had written about practically everything, and his comic devices were easy to fall into. White once showed me something he'd written and asked anxiously, "Did Benchley say that?" In a 1933 preface I said that we were all afraid that whatever we were engaged in had probably been done better by Robert Benchley in 1924.

Benchley beat me to a lot of things, including the Algonquin pigeons and the *Eclaireur* of Nice, whose murky cuts he said were "presumably etched on pieces of bread." His day dreamer, cool and witty on the witness stand (1935) and in heroic peril (1932) antedated a little old day dreamer of my own named Mitty. This is Bob's dreamer, in 1932:

"It usually ends by your making yourself the hero on an imaginary wreck at sea, on this very ship, perhaps. You are sitting right where you are now, when the terrifying news comes that the ship is sinking. Calmly you slip your book into your pocket, button your coat about you and light a cigarette (or better yet, a pipe). You even allow yourself to become slightly British on this occasion, for British men are more the type.

"This mysterious stranger, who has been sitting alone the entire voyage ('I looked over his shoulder once and he was reading Hazlitt,' one of the survivors will report), becomes a tower of strength on the sinking ship, encouraging women here, assisting the crew there, and, with a wry little smile, jesting with the children as he lifts them into the lifeboats. If you had not already been in evening dress, it

149

would be a rather fine gesture to go below and put it on for the last Great Adventure."

It got harder and harder for Benchley to write, and he gave it up before he was fifty, but he had done five hundred pieces. Of one of the last he said, "It was written in blood, I can tell you that." He left behind a rich legacy of humor, comedy, satire, parody, and criticism—all rolled into one in those thirty-five magnificent movie shorts—but he didn't think he was very good at anything.

"Being simply a person who writes little articles sporadically, and with no distinction," he once wrote, "I am always forced to have something in mind about which to write." We all heard him say this, in paraphrase, a dozen times.

The heavier critics have underrated Benchley because of his "short flight," missing his distinguished contribution to the fine art of comic brevity. He would thank me not to call him an artist, but I think he was an artist who wouldn't give up to it, like a busy housewife fighting the onset of a migraine headache.

It was an artist, to cite outstanding proof, who wrote that brilliant and flawless parody of Galsworthy called "The Blue Sleeve Garter." He had all the equipment for the "major flight," but he laid it aside to lead one of the most crowded private lives of our century. Even so, he somehow found time to work on an ambitious enterprise, a book about the satirists of the Queen Anne period, which he later turned into a history in play form. For all its seriousness, it seems to have been a kind of monumental hobby, and a man is never done with a hobby. Benchley didn't finish his.

In all Benchley, a fresh wind stirs in every page. In all his books, you find him ducking swiftly, looking closely, writing sharply.

I have space for a few gleams and swatches:

"This God-given talent which I have must be tossed aside like an old mistress (or is it mattress?)."

"He is a little man who has difficulty in breathing (not enough, however)."

"There was a big bull-pigeon walking about on the window ledge and giving me an occasional leer with its red eyes."

"Sun shining on closed eyelids (on my closed eyelids) soon induces large purple azaleas whirling against a yellow background."

"At a hundred yards he could detect a purple wolf's cup (or Lehman's dropsy) and could tell you, simply by feeling a flower in the dark, which variety of bishop's ulster it was."

"Working on the piece-system as we do (so much per word or per piece—or perhaps)."

"The London illustrated weeklies are constantly making remarkable discoveries in the Etruscan-tomb belt."

I could go on till dusk.

Benchley has been placed in the Leacock "school," but this is too facile a classification. For just one thing, Benchley did more funny things in, and to, banks than Stephen ever dreamed of. Leacock was an "I" writer and Benchley, even in the first person, a "You" writer. Leacock is Leacock, but Benchley's Mr. Ferderber is practically every man.

Comparison is easy. A facet of the Benchley fancy resembles the comic approach of the late Max Adeler, but I never heard him mention the Comparable Max—or Leacock, either. To most of us, he stands alone, in a great, good place all his own. He died at fifty-six, to the grief and dismay of us all, but what he left is Robert Charles Benchley, unique, complete, and in the round.

The warm memory of Bob Benchley that each of his thousand friends will always have is larger and stronger than any memorial a man could touch with his hands. We think of him a lot. I find myself whistling that old song he liked from "Little Jesse James." I remember him brightening hotel lobbies and those other public places which, as Gibbs says, "have the simple merit of staying open all night." He wasn't an outdoors man (he said he could spot only the carnation and the robin), and he accepted daytime with many reservations. He liked to sit the night out in a lighted room with friends.

When he died, one of them said, "They're going to have to stay up late in heaven now." Yes, they're staying up late, I know, and, what is more, they must be having the time of their infinities. Lucky angels.

September, 1949

19

"Scott in Thorns"

ᴽᴽᴽᴽᴽᴽᴽᴽᴽᴽᴽᴽᴽᴽᴽᴽᴽᴽᴽᴽᴽᴽᴽ

As a writer who occasionally does pieces requiring research, I am familiar, on a minor scale, with the kind of problems that must have confronted F. Scott Fitzgerald's biographer when he began, some years ago, to try "to make Scott clear," as Hemingway puts it in one of the notes in Arthur Mizener's *The Far Side of Paradise*. The researcher lives a new life, more complicated than his old one. Interviews with informed sources, male and female, lead to hangover or friendship, both of which take up time; important clipings in scrapbooks have been torn in two by somebody's little niece; the person you most want to talk to is on a West Indies cruise, or hunting in Africa, or mute with laryngitis; the gentleman who gave you the item or anecdote you prize above all others calls up and pleads with you not to use it; the most fascinating notes and letters turn out to be as hard to get your hands on as the private papers of Geoffrey Aspern; and at least one man wants to sock you, and one woman threatens to sue you and your publisher if you mention her—or if you don't.

Mr. Mizener must have gone through a lot of things

153

like this in his long labor of love, but his interest remained remarkably fresh and intense, and I am impressed by that, and by his skillful organization of a mountain of data and details. If there sometimes seems to be almost too much material, so that it becomes hard to tell the facts from the truth, I am sure the author threw out twice as much stuff as he finally included, in a book that is not only biography and criticism but what amounts to an exciting and fast-moving novel about the most colorful and crowded marriage of the Crazy Twenties, a period many of us once prayed we might survive, and to which we would now gladly return, as if it were a warm and serene womb of time. It is this feeling, natural enough in an era of desperation, that probably accounts for the fact that the Mizener book soon began to move like a fictional best seller.

I say "crowded" marriage, because there were four or five Zeldas and at least eight Scotts, so that their living room was forever tense with the presence of a dozen disparate personalities, even when they were alone in it. Some of these Fitzgeralds were characters out of a play or a novel, which made the lives of the multiple pair always theatrical, sometimes unreal, and often badly overacted. They had a flair for destructive wit and exhausting extravaganza, but they were rarely relaxed enough for true comedy or comfortable enough for genuine humor, and they seemed to move dramatically, from the beginning, in settings designed for tragedy. In even their most carefree moments and their most abandoned moods there was scarcely ever the casual ring of authentic gaiety. The "dead-earnest" husband and the frantic wife, to name only two of them, did not know how to invite gaiety. They twisted its arm, got it down, and sat on its chest.

Mr. Mizener brought to his study of Fitzgerald the sensibility, taste, and discretion of a devoted admirer, but "to make Scott clear" he had to report, I suppose, many of the old familiar eccentricities and violences of his subject. These stick out like the peaks of icebergs, more startling than significant, indicating, but never fully revealing, the complex, submerged personality that impulsively thrust them into view. Scott Fitzgerald will be remembered, I am afraid, as The Great Drinker of the Jazz Era, but he was not, I stubbornly insist, a natural alcoholic in the same way, for example, that Joe DiMaggio was a natural ball player. He began to use liquor for posture and gesture, like almost any other writer of the 1920's, but by the time he was forty he had found or invented ten or twelve reasons for keeping it up. (Most writers have only four or five.) The most persistent of these was that his creative vitality demanded stimulation if it was to continue to operate. His earlier tendency to turn to alcohol because of Zelda's tragedy, his constant financial worries, his conviction that he was a failure, his disillusionment about The Kingdom of the Very Rich, and his sorrow over the swift passing of youth and romantic love, was not pathologically compulsive, and I think he could have overcome it. But when Fitzgerald began to drink because he thought he had to, in order to write, he was lost. At the very end, however, he gave it up to work, slowly and painfully but surely and brilliantly, on the novel that many critics believe would have been his finest.

I can think of no genuine alcoholic who could have gone as far as he did and ever have found his way back. To him Ring Lardner was The Great Drinker, and he seemed ruefully surprised that Hemingway insisted on viewing *him* in the same light. Hemingway once wrote him a letter in which he said, "Of course you're a rummy. But you're no

155

more of a rummy than Joyce is and most good writers are. . . ." The saga of Fitzgerald's bats and benders runs all through the Mizener book, but I doubt if we know enough about drinking and drinkers to classify or define Fitzgerald with absolute certainty. To prove to myself how hard it is to classify drinkers, I dashed off, one afternoon, my own personal definitions of a few of the more famous categories of bibulous men. Nobody, I imagine, will agree with me, but here they are, anyway.

The Rummy. He has several suits, but always puts the brown one back on when he gets up in the afternoon. (Fitzgerald was neat and fastidious.) He is inclined to be friendly rather than obnoxious, and likes to tell you that he gets more done and feels better than he did in his sober years. He is given to humming.

The Drunk. He is the stranger who annoys your party as you're leaving "21." He has no name. He appears from nowhere and reels off in the direction of nothing. He talks to himself.

The Drunken Bum. Same as The Drunk, except that he asks for money, or falls down, or both. He curses.

The Souse. He drinks the way other men play cards or bet on the horses. He always stands at the bar, and will not sit in a booth. He has the lowdown on everything, and loves to talk about his wife, and sports. The more he drinks the shrewder he becomes, and he is a hard man to roll, to cheat at cards, or to lure into the badger game. He could find his way home blindfolded on the darkest night of the year. He loves to sing in a male quartet.

The Sot. He always sits alone at a table in a corner, doesn't know where he is or who you are, and doesn't want to be told. He has had the prettiest girls and the toughest luck of anybody in the world. He calls everybody Jack. He likes to play one song on the juke box over and over, as many as thirty times.

The Inebriate. He calls The Drunk "My man," and tells him to "be off." He has gray hair, half a dozen topcoats and canes, and a silk hat. He has invented a fancy mixed drink of his own and sticks to it. He likes to tell how he got the better of some eminent official in Washington. He enjoys only classical music.

I met Scott Fitzgerald only once, but it was a long meeting that began at ten o'clock in the evening and lasted until after seven the following morning. I think it was early

April, and I know it was 1934, because *Tender Is the Night* was just about to be published, and Zelda was having a show of her paintings in New York, and Mizener's book says that it was held during April of that year. Scott was going on forty then, and my first glimpse of him was when he stepped up to the bar in Tony's famous kitchen on Fifty-second Street and ordered a drink. The collar of his topcoat was turned up rakishly on one side and his hat, which he kept on, was pulled down jauntily over one eye. It was an almost studied effect, but it was oddly contradicted by Fitzgerald's curious air of self-disapproval. He seemed to stare at himself in the mirror behind the bar as if he were the awkward "peasant" from the Middle West that he used to claim to be when he talked about the Very Rich.

I had always wanted to meet him—most writers of the twenties had, and still have, a strong affection for F. Scott Fitzgerald, whether they knew him or not. When Tony brought him over to where I was sitting, and mumbled my name, Fitzgerald said, flatly, "Why should I talk to you?" I explained that I was a Middle Western writer hammering briskly away in my tiny corner of literature, and he snarled at Tony, "Why don't you get names right?" and sat down. He was, during the next five hours, witty, forlorn, pathetic, romantic, worried, hopeful, and despondent, but the Scott Fitzgerald I met was quiet and pleasant, too, and not difficult. When two big guys, not unlike the Killers in Hemingway's story, walked past our table and, as luck would have it, one of them said something disparaging about Ernest, my companion rose dramatically to his feet and said to them, "I am Scott Fitzgerald." Before he could ask them to apologize, they muttered something and walked away. This was as close as he came to the edge of trouble that night, and I should like to report that of the four or five eminent writers of the Crazy Decade with whom I have spent the night hours drinking, Scott was the best behaved, the least menacing, and the quietest, and he held his liquor better than any of the others.

That was just one Scott, on only one night, to be sure, but it is the way I will always think of him. To some of his friends he was "extremely difficult," or "a bad child," but a man I talked to recently said, fondly, "He was a sweet guy." Each of us had his different Scott Fitzgerald. If Zelda had completely recovered in that lovely springtime, and if his novel had been well received by the critics, I think he would never have turned to the destructive drinking of straight gin and might be alive today, writing steadily, and

158

possibly lecturing the rest of us on the advantages of moderation and the inner check. But he never had any luck.

When I mentioned *The Great Gatsby*, which I had read three times, he snapped, "I don't want to talk about that book, I want to talk about my Testament of Faith." By this he meant *Tender Is the Night*, the writing of which had taken a heavy toll of his vitality. He told me that his hostess at a recent party in Virginia had brought him a copy of *The Great Gatsby* and asked him to inscribe it for her. "I will never write my name again in any book except my Testament of Faith," he told her coldly. It was one of those theatrical moments which Fitzgerald, the actor, could bring to such a high and embarrassing point. The situation fortunately had been saved when the lady squealed, "Oh, I surely must have *that* book of yours!" and rushed to her library to ransack its shelves for *Testament of Faith,* by F. Scott Fitzgerald.

He had in his pockets that night at Tony's at least three dozen of the catalogues of Zelda's show, whose most arresting canvas, I found out later, was a sharp, warm, ironic study of her husband's handsome and sensitive profile, which she had called "Scott in Thorns." By midnight I must have had a dozen of these in my own pockets because he kept absently handing them to me. At three o'clock in the morning, the hour he made famous, he suddenly said, "Do you know any good girl we could call on?" I got up and went to the telephone, although I was all for keeping the party stag. The first two good girls I called exclaimed, identically, "You and Scott Fitzgerald both at this hour? You must think I'm crazy." The third good girl I reached was an actress, who had not yet gone to bed, and she said, "Give me half an hour." Thirty minutes later—the drinking gentleman is meticulous in these matters late at night

—we arrived at her apartment building and the night elevator man phoned up to say, "Mr. Fitzwater and Mr. Thurman to see you." We were indignant, but we took the gross insult in our dignified stride.

The next few hours were spent in tranquil conversation about a great many things. Most of the time I sat in another room, since it was he who had wanted to talk to a good girl. I understand that this was the year that Fitzgerald made several pathetically futile attempts to interest himself in other women, in an effort to survive the mental and emotional strain of Zelda's recurring psychotic states. In one of the stories that he wrote for the *Saturday Evening Post* later that year, the name of his heroine was the same as that of his hostess of the April morning. But it didn't mean much to him, because all that night Zelda was in his lap, and there were a million miles between him and the good girl who sat only a few feet away.

He was staying at the Algonquin, and he kept forgetting that I had a room there, too. When we drove up in front of the hotel in bright daylight, he got out and said to me, "You don't really belong to my generation and you don't have a daughter." These were two of his great obsessions, and he must not have been listening earlier when I told him my age and talked about my own daughter. "I am less than two years older than you," I told him, "and I have a daughter." He got back in the cab and told the driver to drive around the park. This trip lasted an hour, and we talked about a writer who was much older than either one of us and who didn't have a daughter, the late Ring Lardner, of whom his young friend Scott later said, "He had a face like a cathedral." When I got up late that afternoon, I found that I had at least two dozen catalogues of Zelda's show in my pockets. Later, when I talked to the good girl who had taken us in the night before, she said, "I have about ten catalogues of his wife's show. He kept handing them to me all the time."

The sentimental notion, currently so popular, that Fitzgerald's name began to fade in the 1930's and that he was completely lost to literary view after his death, and had to be revived by Mizener and, indirectly, by Budd Schulberg, simply does not stand up under examination. In 1945 Viking brought out *The Portable Fitzgerald* in a series devoted, in large part, to his living contemporaries, and not to resurrected ghosts, and in the same year that fascinating and widely reviewed book about him called *The Crack-Up*, edited by his friend Edmund Wilson, appeared; in 1948 the Columbia Broadcasting System's excellent *Studio One* dramatized *The Last Tycoon* in an hour-long performance that was lovingly done, excited much comment, and showed the strength and fineness of this unfinished book; and in the summer of 1949 the latest Hollywood remake of *The Great Gatsby* opened in New York. Malcolm Cowley and Alfred Kazin and a dozen other critics had been exploring and re-exploring Fitzgerald well before the so-called "revival," and there were countless other signs that he had not fallen into precocious neglect. For one thing, his name has remained bright and constant in the writings and conversations of American writers who can forget a man quickly enough when his time has come.

Much is now being made of the fact that *Tender Is the Night* sold only thirteen thousand copies. (A much later edition reached almost half a million, I am told.) It so happened that Fitzgerald's books never were runaway best sellers, and Mizener notes that even *This Side of Paradise* had a remarkably moderate success for so famous a novel. It sold only about fifty thousand copies in three years. The

161

infinitely better and far more readable *Gatsby* did not reach thirty thousand in its first twelve months, four years before the depression. A fair analysis of the comparative sales of *Tender Is the Night* would have to take into consideration the taste of the American reading public in 1934. I can't go into this in any great detail, but it is interesting to point out that two tremendous sellers of that year and the year before, *Goodbye, Mr. Chips* and *Anthony Adverse,* were well at the top of the list.

It is true that the critical reception of *Tender Is the Night* profoundly depressed its author, but many critics who reviewed it unfavorably have since revised their estimates upward, and Hemingway, on whose judgment Fitzgerald greatly depended, said in 1935 that the book seemed much better to him that it had when he first read it. As for all the talk about Fitzgerald's books having been out of print when he died in 1940, it should be remembered that this was a good six years after the publication of his last novel. Even the most popular books do not have a way of staying in print very long in a country of fickle and restless tastes that goes in for the Book of the Month, the Man of the Year, and the Song of the Week.

The good and simple truth is that Fitzgerald never disappeared into a lonely literary limbo. I am sorry if this fact disturbs the dreams of the careless romantics who like to believe that a quiet oblivion somehow sweetly suits the short, unhappy life of the "Symbol of the Twenties."

The stature of the writing Fitzgerald, the best of all the Fitzgeralds, has undergone many distortions, from emotional magnification to the sort of cold mental dissection that misses or minimizes his warm understanding, his indestructible honesty, the fine perception that always, in the end, saw through the illusions that plagued him, the charm

162

of his "jeweled prose," and the literary grace and artistic soundness that were born in him. He thought of his talent as something that could be lost, like his watch, or mislaid, like his hat, or slowly depleted, like his bank account, but in his last year there it still was, perhaps surer and more mature than it had ever been. This is a happy thing to remember.

April, 1951

20

The Man Who Was Comedy

I caught my first glimpse of George S. Kaufman a long time ago, during the run of *Dulcy*, and my last glimpse of him in 1933 at a big party given by Howard Dietz, the kind of party of which it is said, "Everybody was there." I passed him on the stairs, as I was going up to the men's room and he was coming down, and we smiled and nodded, and that was all. Still, he remains a vivid page in my album of mental photographs. He looked, I thought, harried, lonely and far-away.

It was a gay party, made up of what I might call impromptu vaudeville turns, starring, informally, Beatrice Lillie, Libby Holman, Harold Ross, and a score of other figures in the theatre and the arts, but George Kaufman never projected himself in such a gathering. He could teach an actor or actress how to project, but he had no gift or desire for it himself. As the evening progressed and the gaiety heightened, I caught one more glimpse of him before he disappeared. He stood in the corner of the big living room, harried, lonely, and far-away, silently listening to an actress who was clearly pouring out her woes in an

164

endless harangue. I truly believe that the only person who ever caught more than glimpses of George Kaufman was George Kaufman himself, and it is a pity that he did not put himself on paper in an autobiography, but it is also unimaginable that he would have done so.

He did write about himself, obliquely and humorously, in a dozen pieces for *The New Yorker*, the first of which appeared in 1935 and the last in 1960, when he was seventy. It was a memoir of Irving Berlin, who wrote the music for the Marx brothers' *Cocoanuts,* for which Kaufman did the book. (He was even collaborating on a play with Leueen MacGrath during his last year.) He also wrote three poems for *The New Yorker,* one of them called "Lines After a Month in the Hospital." But all these were glimpses of Kaufman, and in no sense a revelation of his inner self. The middle 1930's seem to have been an Up Phase in his life, for it was not until 1936 that he joined The Players. He dropped his membership in the club ten years later. Unlike some of us, including Marc Connelly and me, to name two, who will perform in public at the drop or non-drop of a hat, he was not a performer, although he did appear briefly, and was very funny, too, in the role of a frustrated writer in Hollywood in *Once in a Lifetime.* His appearance in an office or a living room instantly attracted attention, an attention that he did not encourage. I never saw him at "21," the old Tony's, or Bleeck's, favorite haunts of most of his theatre and newspaper colleagues.

This "theatre giant," as one of the New York newspapers properly called him in its front-page obituary, deserves a biography. Ben Hecht wrote about Charles MacArthur, Samuel Hopkins Adams did Alexander Woollcott, and I myself tried to capture on paper what I could of Harold Ross, but the lack of a book about Kaufman leaves a serious gap in the written history of the Broadway theatre. When Bob Benchley died, his old friend Donald Ogden Stewart wrote me, "Benchley *was* humor." It could be said, with equal truth, that Kaufman *was* comedy. The wit for which he was so justly famous often tended to obscure rather than to illuminate the man and his achievements. He was a born newspaperman, as his friend and colleague Brooks Atkinson has pointed out, more at home and happier at his typewriter in his office at the *Times* than anywhere else. Yet the span of George Kaufman's active years in the theatre was, in large part, the very measure of the rise of Broadway comedy, which seemed to decline as he withdrew from it. He was, as everybody has emphasized, eminently a collaborator, with such distinguished co-workers as Connelly, Edna Ferber, Moss Hart, Herman Mankiewicz, and several others. It reminds me of Alfred Goullet, once described by "Iron Man" MacNamara as the greatest six-day bike rider that ever lived. In six-day racing you have to have a collaborator, and Goullet rode with most of them. Teamed with him, they almost never lost.

There have been carping critics, such as George Jean Nathan, who saw George Kaufman mainly as a gag man, a slick contriver of stage comedies, a skillful director, and this notion was actually helped out by his own sardonic and skeptical attitude toward Broadway. This attitude, like Harold Ross's notorious gruffness, covered up a far deeper feeling, however. The writer of humor and comedy is by nature a complicated human being, and the craft he practices is in part a necessary counterbalance to God knows how many different kinds of inner conflicts.

Booth Tarkington, a master of humor and comedy in and out of the theatre, said of *Dulcy* that it was "one of the gayest comedies I ever saw." I saw this Kaufman-Connelly
166

play several times in 1921 because, for one thing, I was an old friend of Elliott Nugent, who appeared in it. The influence of a man like George Kaufman on aspiring writers of comedy for the theatre is an imponderable factor, but I believe that the success of *Dulcy* gave Nugent a real boost when, the following year, he wrote *Kempy* with his father, and then, in 1925, *The Poor Nut*. *Dulcy* was also one of my own inspirations, and so was the Kaufman-Connelly play *Merton of the Movies*. In the early 1920's I came to New York once a year and took in sixteen plays, which I reviewed for a Sunday half page that I conducted in the Columbus (Ohio) *Dispatch*. I can still remember, after nearly four decades, a sentence I wrote in 1923 about *Merton of the Movies*. It went like this: "I think that I shall never forget the book scene in the first act and the love scene in the last." Marc Connelly's contributions to *Dulcy* and to *Merton* cannot be overestimated, and Kaufman was lucky and happy in a collaborator of warmth, brilliance, and a rare talent for comic invention.

Kaufman could say, in one of his flashes of wit, "Satire is what closes on Saturday night," but his contribution to the American comedy theatre in the field of satire was considerable. With Connelly he more than kidded the movies, and with Moss Hart he continued this hilarious assault. He also took in his sardonic stride politics, government, the Supreme Court, big business, and the theatre. It would therefore be completely wrong and misleading to take at face value George Kaufman's offhand, often defensive and cynical dismissal of his own gifts.

When I was writing *The Years with Ross,* I kept remembering the scores of times the founder of *The New Yorker* had spoken appreciatively of Kaufman's wisdom and good sense. One of the things his old friend had said to Ross,

167

years ago, was, "Now the backers want to *read* the script." Kaufman's years on Broadway started with the era in which any backer would rush his money into a Kaufman collaboration sight unseen, and ended in the present desperate financial condition of the theatre, which caused a friend of mine to write me recently in London, "For God's sake get back here and prevent me from putting any money in any play at all."

During my writing of the Ross book, the warmest and most moving letters I got about Ross, and about my pieces in the *Atlantic Monthly,* came from Kaufman. The wit still flashed in these letters, but on paper it did not obscure, it illuminated the New York scene, with something far deeper than the verbal dart throwing that characterized the "old gang," as George called the members of the Algonquin Round Table. As long ago as 1927 Marc Connelly and I were on first-name terms with each other, but it wasn't until my last two or three letters to Kaufman, and his replies, that we became George and Jim. I shall always be thankful for that, and I shall forever cherish one note in particular. I had written a chapter on Ross and sex and love. Kaufman had known Ross longer than most of us (since 1918) and his words were a masterpiece of highly exaggerated praise: "Your current piece in the *Atlantic* ('Sex Is an Incident') is the best piece ever written about anybody, by anybody, at any time." And this from the man of whom it was once so falsely said that he had a mind but not a heart!

The legend of George Kaufman will grow; the truth about the man himself will probably stay just where it is, but time will brighten the light he brought to American humor, comedy, and wit. If the theatre is to have a renascence of comedy, it will need another Kaufman, and

168

the need is extremely great in the present period of deca-
dence, in which we do not seem to be able to tell the differ-
ence between *avant-garde* and *fin de siècle,* talent and
sickness, the giving up of taboos and the breaking down
of morals, the experimental and the expiring theatre.

After my fashion, when I wake up at dawn, I try to dis-
tract my mind from the woes of the world by paraphrasing
verses, and it was only the other morn that I thought of
this one in connection with George S. Kaufman:

> Yesteryear upon the stair,
> I met a man who wasn't there.
> He wasn't there again today.
> I wish he hadn't gone away.

21

M_y Friend McNulty

The angel that writes names in a book of gold must long ago have put McNulty down as one who delighted in his fellow man. His delight in human beings was warm and deep and, though he deserved to be called a social critic, he was concerned mainly with men, not Man, with persons, not People. McNulty's love of humanity was not expressed at a distance, from a platform, but in pieces that have the lasting pulse of life in every sentence. He moved among men, shoulder to shoulder, from morning till night until the end of his too brief sixty years on earth.

American writing in our time has developed few men with so keen an eye and so sharp an ear. Nothing, however commonplace, that he touched with words remained commonplace, but was magnified and enlivened by his intense and endless fascination with the stranger in the street, the drinker at the bar and the bartender behind it, the horse player, the cab driver, the guy at the ball game, the fellow across the room, the patient in the next hospital bed. John McNulty, city man and newspaperman, self-assigned in his mature years to human-interest stories of the world about him, left not only a body of work that throbs with his love of life but a vast and equally durable legacy of spoken words that remain vivid in the memory of his friends. The only person who could get McNulty down in words was McNulty himself, but those of us who knew and loved him like to sit around at night in Tim and Joe Costello's Bar and Restaurant on Third Avenue and talk about him. This is the only real way to bring McNulty to life. Cold type could never do justice to such a man.

After John McNulty died, I wrote a short piece about him for the crowded pages of *The New Yorker*, and I reproduce it here in part: "Nobody who knew McNulty as man or writer could ever have confused him for a moment with anybody else. His presence in a room—or in a town, for that matter—was as special as the way he put words down on paper. His death darkened the skies for literally countless friends and acquaintances, for he seemed to know everybody. He came back to New York in the early thirties from a long sojourn in the Middle West, and in 1937 he began writing pieces for *The New Yorker*. They were the reports of a true and eager eye and ear that found high excitement in both the unusual and the common phrases and postures of men, and turned them into the sparkle of his unique idiom.

"The days didn't go by for John McNulty; they happened to him. He was up and out at six every morning, wandering the beloved streets and 'avenyas' of his city, stopping to talk and listen to everybody. His week was a seven-day circus that never lost its savor. He was not merely an amusing companion; he was one of the funniest of men. When he told a tale of people or places, it had a color and vitality that faded in the retelling by anyone else. The name McNulty, for us, meant 'Inimitable,' and at the same

171

time something in lower case, familiar and cherished—a kind of synonym for laughter. We grieve that such a man cannot be replaced, in our hearts or on our pages."

The pages of *The New Yorker* sparkled with his pieces from the first one, which appeared on Christmas Day, 1937, until the last one, which was printed on New Year's Eve, 1955.

McNulty and I were reporters together on Columbus, Ohio, newspapers in the early 1920's. He did general assignments for a morning paper while I covered City Hall for an afternoon paper, but our offices were just a few blocks apart, in the center of town, and I bumped into him almost every day, often at the corner of Broad and High streets, the city's main intersection. He was invariably excited about something, the cabin lights of the Shenandoah which he had seen twinkling in the sky the night before, a girl at the James Theatre who sang "Roses Are Shining in Picardy," Donn Byrne's novel *The Changelings*, which he demanded that I begin reading right away, there on that crowded corner, or a song called "Last Night on the Back Porch" which he insisted on playing for me, then and almost there. Actually, he took me around the corner to a music store and began beating out the song on the first piano he came to, to the astonishment of the store's staff. "It's McNulty," I explained to them in a whisper and they all nodded and breathed his name in unison, obviously believing that he was a great pianist, come to play at Memorial Hall, who had suddenly been seized by a rare moment of relaxation and frivolity. He had once played the piano in a movie theatre in the days of silent films and, within his range, there wasn't anything he couldn't make the keys do. While playing "My Gal Sal" he used to recite the succession to the presidency, and it was upon the conclusion of that bravura performance that we

172

left the music shop and its startled and transfigured staff. Once he got me up before breakfast to play on my Victrola two records that had entranced him—"Singin' Sam from Alabam'" and a bright arrangement of "Everybody Calls Me Honey," in which piano, trumpet, and banjo alternately took over the solo.

McNulty was a widely experienced newspaperman at twenty-five, when he arrived in Columbus from the East, to work for the *Ohio State Journal* at sixty dollars a week, higher pay than any reporter in town had been getting. I have forgotten, if I ever knew, what whim or compulsion had sent him into the Middle West. It was probably an impulse peculiar to his volatile spirit, such as that which sent him one day, years later, to New Iberia, Louisiana, to visit the tabasco factory there. In Columbus he lingered for a dozen years. Before the first of these had passed he knew more people in the city than I did, although I had been born and brought up there. They included everybody from taxi drivers, cops, prizefighters, and bellboys to the mayor of the city and the governor of the state. He wrote speeches for one successful candidate for governor, and in that, as in everything else, he had the time of his life.

John once explained to me, "Two thirds of the Irish blood is grease paint," and he was a fine offhand actor and raconteur rampant, who would jump from his chair in a living room and theatrically bring to life one of the characters he had so fondly collected during his wanderings. I think he did as much as anyone, with his acting, to ridicule the Ku Klux Klan out of existence in Columbus. He had arranged for me to accost him whenever I saw him at Broad and High in the company of a group of men—he was always surrounded by men—and loudly try to enroll him in the Klan. "We are looking for likely one hundred percent Americans," I would say, "so we can build up in this city the biggest Kleagle in the country."

"Klavern," he would correct me, and while his companions stared at me in disbelief, he would take off his hat, present to me the shining map of Ireland that was his face, and say proudly, "The name is John Aloysius McNulty." At this I would slink away, muttering, while his friends stared after me. "Them guys must be crazy!" I heard a boxer named Sully exclaim after one of these rituals, and the word got around town that the local Klan was made up of imbeciles. It didn't last long.

Trying to describe McNulty is a little like trying to describe Ed Wynn or George M. Cohan. "A small, jaunty man, best described as Irish of face and manner" is the way the *New York Times* went about it in that paper's appreciative obituary. He was small, I guess, measured by physical height and weight, but I have a tendency to look up when I think of him, for to me he was nine feet tall. This was the stature, at any rate, of his unflagging comic spirit. The dictionary has no exact words for the face and voice of the man, or for the shape and color of the moods he put on every morning with his clothes. There was nothing of the literary elf about McNulty, who once said to me, "Only people with Vincent for a middle name write about leprechauns." It is true that the world of John McNulty bordered on Oz and Wonderland, but it consisted mainly of Ireland, New York's Third Avenue, the city rooms of American newspapers, and the race tracks of the world, with many an odd and unexpected nook and corner. From the border states came curious and wondrous figures, attracted to McNulty, not magically, but naturally. This gave his world, and his comments on it, a strange truth, undreamed of in ordinary philosophies. When he said, of 1885, "That was the year the owls were so bad," or when
174

he told a lady trying to think of her hairdresser's name, "Girls named Dolores become hairdressers," or when he tracked down a bookie in a jewelry shop by suddenly remembering "All watch repairers are named Schneider," the listener felt that this was not mere whimsy but McNulty fact. There was always, faint or sharp, in what he said or did a critical comment on our tangled civilization, a sound parody of the ways of men. Walking about the streets of any city with McNulty was to be taken on a guided tour of what William James called, in another context, unexplored experience. Two men would pass by you, one of them saying, "It's the biggest gorilla in the world. They call it Garganetta," or a waiter in a café would tell him, "We get stranglers come in here at all hours." Through the ears of many of us such things pass unregistered, but McNulty's sensitized mind recorded everything. "The lady was a Bostonian, they call them" rang like a bell in his consciousness. To a man whose awareness was always on the lookout for the unusual, as well as the typical, the world was a book he was reading with intense concentration. He loved sentiment, being Irish, and he came right out with it. Of a pretty young bride he once wrote about in the *Daily News* he said, "She was as cute as a little red wagon." He once called me long distance to tell me he had just read something lovely which I had to hear. It was the four words of a lover: "My eyes desire you." My phone brought me often, but not often enough, phrases, sentences, or paragraphs from an enthusiastic McNulty who had just stumbled upon them. Sometimes he read me a whole piece.

There were a dozen shops of all kinds on New York's East Side with whose proprietors McNulty, making his daily rounds, kept up some kind of running gag. Once when I lived on East Fifty-seventh Street, a region he knew well, he took me into a small corner store after explaining, "There's a wonderful guy runs this place." He was a wonderful guy, too, in the McNulty tradition, perfectly suited to their particular running gag, which was managed deadpan, as if the two had never met before. "What can I do for you, sir?" the man said. McNulty consulted the back of an envelope. "Elephant goad," he said finally. An amateur actor of McNulty's stripe, the man began snapping his fingers, humming, and searching his shelves and opening doors underneath the shelves, at length turning around to report, "Sorry, seem to be fresh out of elephant goads. Anything else?" McNulty shook his head sorrowfully and out we went. I found out later, dropping into the shop, some of the other things McNulty had asked for in vain— fetlock cleaners, beagle harness, and noiseless dice. "He says he supplies dice to a couple of fugitives holed up in this house with marble floors," the proprietor said. This is the thinnest ice of comedy and it takes experts to skate on it without falling in. You had to behold such performances yourself to understand the skill of McNulty and his stooges. I have never read a critic who captured the subtle essence of Beatrice Lillie's comic art, and none of them could do justice to McNulty's, either, on flat paper. His timing was perfect, and so were the tricks of his tones of voice. One day a few years ago I phoned him to ask if he remembered the year he had interviewed Donald Ogden Stewart (a great McNulty admirer) for the *Ohio State Journal*. McNulty's answer was prompt, and in the tone of a professional quiz panelist. "It was the year Black Gold win the Derby," he said, and having given me all the help a true horseplayer should need, he hung up. I had to look up in the World Almanac the year Black Gold win the Derby. Checking later with the *Journal* files, I found out, of course, that the answer was correct.

176

John Augustine McNulty (Aloysius had been invented for effect) was capable of a fine anger that could rise to fury. Like my own temper, his was sometimes as unreasonable as it was quick, but our occasional disagreements, as sudden as summer storms, passed just as quickly. After one loud hour of argument over the play *Shadow and Substance,* about which I think we were both right, we parted like men who would never see each other again. But we had a running-gag manner of making up, during which the cause of the trouble was never mentioned or even hinted at. Spotting him in a bar, I would present myself, politely, as a man just in from Columbus, Ohio, with a letter to him from Sully. "Let me see the letter," he would say, and there ensued a search through all my pockets, in which he helped. "Let me have another go at your coat," he would say grimly, but the letter was never there. "Well, when you find it," he would say, "bring it around. If I'm not here, I'll probably be somewhere else. Meanwhile, let's have a drink to old Sully." His gallery of persons he disliked was not large, but it included the right figures, the phony, or "wax banana," the snob, the show-off, the blowhard, the bigot, the unfriendly, the humorless, and all their cold ilk.

I happened to be in Columbus in 1933 when McNulty decided to return to the New York he hadn't seen for more than a decade, and I came back on the train with him. We hadn't ridden in a taxi more than three blocks from Pennsylvania Station before he began waving at guys he knew. "You're obvious New York born and bred, Mac," the taxi driver told him, adding that he was studying "human psychology." He picked me as a stranger "from the outlands" and said to my companion, "Better look after your friend. You don't know your way around, it's a tough town." In the next few years McNulty worked on the

177

Mirror, the *Daily News,* and the *Herald Tribune* under its great city editor Stanley Walker, who once told me, "There is a kind of story that only McNulty could write, and it was a pleasure to have him around." He meant the kind of feature story that calls for the use of the heart as well as the mind.

McNulty was a fast writer, but before he reached his typewriter his alert photographic mind, backed up by an amazing memory, had worked the story out in all but a few details. He was temperamental if the thing didn't come out right, but he discarded his temperament like an overcoat when he set out to explore his fascinating world. His first assignment on *The New Yorker* was a "Reporter at Large" piece and he went out, got the facts, came back, and batted out the story within a couple of hours. "He can't get over writing for a newspaper deadline," said the late Harold Ross, but McNulty learned to slow down. When he left for a stint in Hollywood, Ross was genuinely reluctant to see him go. "Well, God bless you, McNulty, goddam it," said Ross. As John told me later, "Ross has two gods, Upper Case and lower case." Through Ross and the rest of us McNulty met a few people he hadn't known before. I remember his delight, one night in "21," when Marc Connelly told him some of Lloyd Lewis's anecdotes about the Southwest, one of which involved a rancher whose cat had been missing for three weeks. "Then one day I turned over my mattress," said the rancher, "and there, between the mattress and the springs, was Boss, pressed as pretty as a flower." The next day McNulty said to me, "The cat's name wasn't Boss. The cat's name was Pete. All ranchers' cats are named Pete." I'm sure Connelly would have lost money betting against this intuitive bit of McNulty truth.

178

McNulty was not New York born, for he first saw the enchanting light of his world in Lawrence, Massachusetts, where his mother ran a little store after the death of his father. Her son has done some justice to these early scenes, but not as much as I wish he had, for his mother is one of the vivid memories of my life. I first met her in Columbus when she visited him there, and he and I went to the train together to see her off, both of us, by coincidence, carrying identical boxes of candy. He knew what to do about that. "If you cry," he told her affectionately, "you get the box of candy that's poisoned. If you're good, you get the other one." The leave-taking was as jolly as it could be when two McNultys parted. Years later in New York, Mrs. McNulty was knocked down by a taxi on Park Avenue, and my wife and I went with John to call on her. Before we could tiptoe into the bedroom, where she was supposed to be lying wrapped in bandages from head to foot, we heard a small clatter in the kitchen and her son went out to investigate. It was Mama, of course. "And did you think I'd let the Thurbers call on me," she said indignantly, "and not fix them a cup o' tea?" It took more than a New York taxi to finish off a McNulty. John himself, although he never talked about it, and wrote about it only sparingly and obliquely, had gone through some of the toughest battles of the First World War, in the Infantry. He got a leg full of shrapnel at Fère-en-Tardenois, and he was made a sergeant when the company's sergeants were killed in battle. After the war, he spent a year in hospital, and his wounds gave him trouble from then on. He was once a pet patient for three weeks in a hospital in Columbus, but none of us knew for a long time that Fère-en-Tardenois had sent him there. He made lasting friendships, of course, with doctors, nurses, and orderlies.

179

A few years before he died he gave me his precious copy of Mencken's *The American Language,* saying, "This is the book I love the most." Mencken once spoke to me, in the Algonquin lobby, in praise of McNulty and his handling of the people and the parlance of Third Avenue, and I remember how McNulty's face lighted up when I told him about it. He had a lot of favorite books, including the Oxford English Dictionary, which he read as if it were a novel filled with wonders and suspense. There must be many of us who have books that McNulty once owned. "He couldn't keep a book he loved," Faith McNulty told me once. "He wasn't happy until he had given it to some friend."

In the last ten years of his life, alas, we ran into each other only occasionally, but we talked a lot on the phone and exchanged letters. His letters were invariably carefully thought out single sentences, each relating some highlight of his city adventures. The last one I ever got was different, though, and puzzled me. It began, as always, "Dear Jimmy," and went on to say, "I think that maybe threescore years and ten is subject to change without notice." I searched it for the laugh, and realized there weren't going to be any more laughs. One night shortly afterward my phone rang in the country and I was told that he was dead. I had been planning to write him suggesting that he read certain poems and pieces by Dylan Thomas, particularly the poem that ends: "They shall have stars at elbow and foot . . . and death shall have no dominion. And death shall have no dominion." But I was too late. If Thomas was right about these bright eternal ornaments, John Augustine McNulty has his stars, and never you mind about that.